Secure Your Retirement Dreams

with $Afe Money

**Build a Retirement Plan That Will Stand the Test of Time
Without Losing Your Money on the Wall Street Roller Coaster**

SECURE YOUR RETIREMENT DREAMS
WITH
$AFE MONEY

**Build a Retirement Plan That Will Stand the Test of Time
Without Losing Your Money on the Wall Street Roller Coaster**

BY

BRENT TYCKSEN

SECURE YOUR RETIREMENT DREAMS WITH SAFE MONEY:
Build a Retirement Plan That Will Stand the Test of Time Without
Losing Your Money on the Wall Street Roller Coaster

Copyright © 2014 by Brent Tycksen

All Rights Reserved

ISBN: 978-1494862855

Printed in the United States of America
Year of First Printing: 2014

Disclaimer: The Publisher and the Author make no representations or warranties with respect to the accuracy or completeness of the contents of this work and specifically disclaim all warranties, including without limitation warranties of fitness for a particular purpose. No warranty may be created or extended by sales or promotional materials. The advice and strategies contained herein may not be suitable for every situation. This work is sold with the understanding that the Publisher is not engaged in rendering legal, accounting, or other professional services. If professional assistance is required, the services of a competent professional person should be sought. Neither the Publisher nor the Author shall be liable for damages arising therefrom.

The fact that an organization or website is referred to in this work as a citation and/or a potential source of further information does not mean that the Author or the Publisher endorses the information the organization or website may provide or recommendations it may make. Further, readers should be aware that Internet websites listed in this work may have changed or disappeared between when this work was written and when it is read. While great efforts have been taken to provide accurate and current information regarding the covered material, neither Brent Tycksen nor Safe Money Associates are responsible for any errors or omissions, or for the results obtained from the use of this information.

To Mom and Dad, for teaching me the value of hard work and the necessity of play.

To my brothers and sister, for your friendship as youth that continues now as we all experience being grandparents, and for being great examples in our entrepreneurial endeavors.

To our four exceptional children, who put up with Dad working long hours.

To our wonderful grandchildren, who love "Papa" and "Grum" unconditionally.

I especially want to thank my wife, who is as beautiful inside as she is outside, and who has put up with me for the forty-two years we have known each other and our thirty-seven years of marriage. You are the love of my life and my eternal companion. You make me want to be a better man. Van ewigheid tot ewigheid.

CONTENTS

FOR SKEPTICS ONLY

What is a Safe Money Retirement Plan? Here's what it isn't: stuffing your money in a mattress or hunkering down with gold bullion. You don't even need to have a million bucks to be in the club. Building a Safe Money Retirement Plan means you've started on a low-risk path that will keep your money safely growing over time—guaranteed. Rest assured, for the average American, the dream of becoming a millionaire is not out of reach. In fact, the blueprint is sitting in your hands right now. Here are some of the most common questions people have had before joining the ranks of building their Safe Money Retirement Plan.

Is it really possible to build a Safe Money Retirement Plan?

Actually, it depends. It's not for everyone. Some people are addicted to the ups and downs of the market—and believe it or not, they can't understand how their money can safely grow each and every day regardless of the economy, market, or latest bad news on TV. If that's you, then sorry—now's the time to shut the cover of this book and pass it on to someone who wants some security and peace of mind in their financial future.

Is it too late for me?

No way! No matter what your age, the concepts embraced by Safe Money professionals can be used to grow and safeguard your money for you or your family at any point in time.

Do I have to scrimp and save and basically eat beans and rice in order to grow my money?

Nope. No dietary changes are required to join the club. In fact, once you discover how to Finance Your Own Prosperity™, you may just end up living better while saving money doing it. There's nothing like living the high life without the heavy dose of guilt or the pressure of a too-tight budget.

Is this just more pop culture investment advice?

This book is for anyone who is sick of the stomach-turning ups and downs of what we like to call the "Wall Street Roller Coaster". The principles taught in this book have been around for years. Case studies range from start-up business owners to the average American household and anywhere in between. If you're sick of the status quo and ready to stop drinking the financial guru Kool-Aid, this book is for you.

Is this just another financial dead end? How do I know whom to trust?

Fortunately for all of us, the solutions we share with you in this book have been around for over a hundred years. In fact, there's a good chance your parents or even grandparents used some of these lost strategies decades ago . . . you might say we're bringing some financial wisdom back from the dead!

Do I need to be a financial whiz?

Not at all. In fact, I think you'll find the whole process refreshingly simple—no monitoring the markets and no complex calculations to worry about. Once you get going, building a Safe Money Retirement Plan can happen almost on autopilot.

Section 1

SAFE: Status Quo Killers

"Status quo, you know—that is Latin for 'the mess we're in.'"
— Ronald Reagan

"Bureaucracy defends the status quo long past the time when the quo has lost its status."
—Dr. Laurence J. Peter

CHAPTER 1

CANCER, CURES, AND KILLING THE STATUS QUO

I am the second-oldest son of six boys and one girl. I was raised by hard-working parents who believed in teaching their children a good, strong work ethic. We had animals, chickens, a vegetable garden, fruit trees, a raspberry patch, and grape vines. We had to care for the animals, milk the goats, gather the eggs, weed and care for our assigned rows in the garden—along with numerous other chores—each and every day. We had to do this before we could go play with our friends. All summer long, we would water, weed, and care for the garden. In the fall, we would pick corn, dig potatoes, dig carrots, and pick apples, peaches, and pears. Then we would help our parents prepare and preserve the harvest by bottling the perishables and putting the potatoes, carrots, apples, and squash into the root cellar properly so they wouldn't spoil.

We were very self-sufficient. We had to be. Although my dad had a good job, we were a large family and didn't have a lot of discretionary income. The literal fruits of our labors would feed us during the winter so we would have funds for new school clothes, shoes, and other necessities.

My parents told us Aesop's Fables and other similar stories on a regular basis. One that I heard a lot was "The Ant and the Grasshopper." It goes like this:

In a field one summer's day, a grasshopper was hopping about, chirping and singing to its heart's content. An ant passed by, bearing along with great toil an ear of corn he was taking to the nest.

"Why not come and chat with me," said the grasshopper, "instead of toiling and moiling in that way?"

"I am helping to lay up food for the winter," said the ant, "and recommend you to do the same."

"Why bother about winter?" said the grasshopper. "We have plenty of food at present." But the ant went on its way and continued its toil.

When the winter came, the grasshopper had no food and found itself dying of hunger, while it saw the ants distributing corn and grain from the stores they had collected in the summer. Then the grasshopper knew: It is best to prepare for the days of necessity.

I remember one time when it was my responsibility to prepare the fresh straw in the bottom of the root cellar so the potatoes, carrots, and apples would not spoil during the long winter. One of my friends came by and encouraged me to hurry so I could go play football with the guys. Instead of replacing all the straw, I just spread a little fresh straw over the top of the old, moist, mildewed straw. From the top, it looked like I had done the job right. But underneath, the mold and mildew had already established a foothold and were infiltrating the new straw. I definitely cut corners so I could go play football with my friends. I don't remember who won the game, but I do remember having to haul out all the rotten potatoes, carrots, and apples in the middle of the winter instead of enjoying them in soups, stews, and pies. My dad took the opportunity to remind me again of the ant and the grasshopper. Unfortunately, as a youth, I was the grasshopper more than I should have been.

As a nineteen-year-old, I had the opportunity to volunteer for two years in southern Africa. Wow, what an eye-opening experience for a young man to live in some of the most technologically advanced countries, and also some of the poorest third-world countries on the planet. In Mozambique and Malawi, starvation and poverty were rampant. Robert Mugabe and his guerilla fighters were terrorizing everyone in Rhodesia (now Zimbabwe). They wanted to take over the government and socialize everything. There would be no rich and no poor. Everyone would have the same amount.

After my two years of service, I returned home, went to school, got married, started a family, and also started several businesses. The teachings of my parents' home were indelibly imprinted on my life. I could be anything I wanted to be, if I was willing to work for it. No one was going to take care of me and my family but me and my family. It's best to prepare for the days of necessity. Oh, yeah . . . work hard and play hard, each at the right time.

My wife and I have been blessed with four wonderful children, and to date, five beautiful grandchildren. We have passed on to them the lessons we learned from our parents and grandparents. In our thirty-seven years of marriage, we have started several successful businesses, and a few that were not as successful. We have always tried to prepare for the days of necessity.

Our first Christmas together, we were poor college students. We gave each other a set of cookware and some food for our pantry. I remember the extravagance of a case of cream of mushroom soup, twenty-four cans of tuna fish, and a ten-pound bag of curly noodles—all part of a family-favorite tuna casserole recipe. Our Christmas present to ourselves helped sustain us as we finished school.

In 2004, I found a lump in my neck. After several diagnostic procedures, we were told that I had stage four thyroid cancer. My thyroid was one giant tumor. The cancer had also spread into my lymph system. I remember the doctor telling us, "I'm not looking for cancer anymore—I'm looking to see how far it has spread." Several weeks later, skilled surgeons removed my thyroid and as many cancerous lymph nodes as they could. After two months of recovery, they started a prolonged radiation treatment regime. Thyroid cancer is slow-growing, so they spread the treatment out over several years. They gave me a high "killer" dose of radiation to destroy as many cancer cells as they could, then let me recover. They used a nuclear medicine scanning device, similar to an MRI, to track where the radiation was being absorbed, to see how far the cancer had spread, and to determine how much had been killed. That was not a fun experience.

The doctor told us that after I ingested the radiation, I needed to stay at least ten feet away from any living thing for two weeks. Those ten feet included through walls, floors, and ceilings. I was banished to a guest room on the top floor of our home, as far away from everyone as possible. We wrapped everything in the room in plastic to protect it so any radioactive body oils, etc. could be disposed of without permanently destroying the item.

Thyroid cells are the only things in our body that will absorb iodine, so oncologists use radioactive iodine to treat thyroid cancer. In order to prepare your body to absorb the iodine, they starve your body of iodine by removing it from your diet and taking you off any thyroid supplements. Thyroid cancer survivors refer to it as "hypo-hell". The thyroid sends out a hormone called T3 that controls how quickly the body uses energy and makes proteins, among other things. Without the T3, you feel like you have a really bad case of influenza. Your body aches, you have no energy, and you are extremely lethargic.

Once the thyroid cells in your body are craving iodine, the doctors give you the radiation treatment. After the treatment, it takes about five months before the flu-like symptoms are completely gone and your energy level somewhat returns. You have about four months of some normalcy, and then they take you off your synthroid (T3) and prepare your body for another dose of radiation . . . and the cycle starts again. After five years of treatments and diagnostic radiation doses and three years in remission, I am an eight-year survivor and officially cancer free.

I'm explaining this in so much detail because in over thirty years as a financial professional, I have seen many people go through this same scenario in their financial lives. They "invest" their funds in something—usually stocks or mutual funds—it functions in some normalcy for the equivalent of four or five months, and then it adjusts or corrects, they lose money, and they have the equivalent of seven or eight months to recover their money. Then they do it all over again. Sometimes the recovery takes four or five years, not months, to get back to where they were. They are in financial "hypo-hell". Their financial health and well-being are devastated by a form of financial cancer. That cancer is investment risk and investment loss. It's eating away at their assets and future stability. The status quo says you have to put your money at risk in order to get gains. And even though people don't like losing their money, they keep doing it over and over again.

An even bigger form of financial cancer is taxes. The government continues to take more and more to provide for larger entitlement programs and "spreading the wealth." Remember Robert Mugabe? He and his guerrillas finally triumphed in Rhodesia and came into power. In Zimbabwe, interestingly enough, everyone does have the same thing now . . . nothing. Once Mugabe got control of the government, he ruled with an iron fist. He raised taxes on the rich to give to the poor. So the rich left. To stop the outflow, he nationalized everything. The large industrialists and farmers left anyway. Food production diminished exponentially. Things that used to be in abundance are now available in limited supply, usually only on the black market because of inflation and devalued currency.

Just like my thyroid cancer, the financial cancers of investment risk, investment loss, and taxes can be defeated. We do not have to let them destroy our planning for our future and retirement. If Aesop were to write an updated version of the ant and the grasshopper, I believe he would also add the caveat to put the fruit of our preparation somewhere that would be safe and protected from loss to assure that it is there for our use in time of want.

How to Kill the Status Quo

Does any of this "status quo" conventional wisdom sound familiar?

1. Diversify with mutual funds.

2. Max out 401(k) contributions.

3. Keep your credit score high, and shop for low interest rates.

4. Buy term and invest the difference.

5. Put your money in the market to get a good rate of return.

6. Defer taxes until later. (The reality that exposes this myth is really going to blow your mind.)

All this sounds good, but how many folks are really getting ahead financially following this advice? The problem is we're often taking advice from people who may actually be keeping the truth from us for their own profit.

We've heard the same old tired commentary from experts, gurus, and TV personalities for years. Their job isn't to make you wealthy. It's to fill air time and sell advertising. In short, they are paid to crank out microwave money content as fast as they can to keep their magazines or air time full.

Likewise, the conventional wisdom preached from the ivory towers of Wall Street was likely never intended to make the average American wealthy. It's engineered for Wall Street's profit.

So, how well has it worked for the average American?

You probably already know the answer because you live it every day. But let's take a look at the proof:

- Half of all households headed by workers aged fifty-five to sixty-four have less than $88,000 in retirement accounts. [1]

- The average American household with at least one credit card has nearly $10,700 in credit card debt. [2]

- Trillions of dollars have evaporated from 401(k) accounts. [3]

- Of those between 45 and 64, 71 percent admit they are worried about having enough money for retirement. [4]

- The average American is paying up to 34.5 percent of their after-tax income straight to interest. [5]

- In 2010, every three months, 250,000 new homes went into foreclosure. [6]

In addition to grappling with increasing expenses and debt, the average American has been devastated by losses in investments. Today, American Associate of Retired

Persons (AARP) estimates 55 million baby boomers are so concerned about the state of their savings that they are keeping tabs on every penny.

The Jaw-dropping Truth about Wall Street

Who *is* getting rich? The Wall Street firms and their executives, that's who. According to the AFL-CIO in 2009, James Dimon of JP Morgan Chase received $9.2 million in compensation, Goldman Sachs's Lloyd Blankfein received $9.8 in compensation, Wells Fargo's John Stumpf received a jaw-dropping $21.3 million, and Bank of America's Thomas Montag received a mind-blowing $29.9 million for one year's worth of compensation. [7]

Now here's the kicker. These are all banks that received money from the government bailout. The list could go on and on. Go back a few more years to 2005. That year, T. Boone Pickens made $1.4 billion. 1.4 *billion* in compensation in *one* year? [8]

Knocks the wind out of you, doesn't it?

Now don't get me wrong—we don't begrudge someone making a fortune for himself. That's what the American Dream is all about. But where does all that money come from to pay those outrageous CEO paychecks?

Is it from manufacturing a product that is sold to a consumer? Is it from building a home, saving a life in a hospital, or selling groceries at the store?

Nope.

It's from Wall Street working the system with their super computers to profit regardless of whether the market goes up or down. The computers and brokerage houses use lightning-fast algorithms to buy and sell millions of shares a day, executing deals within split seconds. These deals can amount to more than 50 percent of trading volume every day.

Is any real value created by these trades, or is it just a great way to make a lot of money at someone else's expense? These folks create fortunes for themselves, while you, the average citizen, could end up riding the roller coaster of market swings with no control over your money.

But lousy investment returns are just the tip of the iceberg. Another problem is how our money flows—in the front door and out the back without stopping to visit. The average American pays up to 34 percent of his after-tax income in interest charges, saving just a small sliver for himself. [9] If you are like most people who refinance their mortgage a couple times throughout their lives, you likely aren't paying that low, advertised interest rate. You could end up paying as much as 80 percent interest on that mortgage! It's a tried-and-true system set up by bankers to ensure you'll keep paying them interest. (This will be explained in Chapter 5, *Killing the Interest Vampire*.)

One infamous quote was recorded when someone saw a massive yacht club full of million-dollar yachts held exclusively for Wall Street executives. "Where are all the c-c-customer's yachts?" he stammered. [10] Good question.

Seems crazy, doesn't it?

It *is* crazy, but that's the status quo.

But that's not you anymore. You're about to discover a whole new world of money because *you* are ready to join the ranks of those able to retire with Safe Money.

There *is* a way to keep a lot more of your money. There *is* a way you can grow wealthy from your hard work—and keep your money safe at the same time. It's easier than you think. The next few chapters are going to show you how not only to kill the status quo, but also how to join the ranks of those able to retire early with Safe Money. To get started, just turn the page!

CHAPTER 2

MY BREAKUP WITH
MR. MARKET

"If I had to give advice, it would be keep out of Wall Street."
— John D. Rockefeller

I have a friend named Ethan Kap. Ethan isn't normal.

You could say he had a strange fascination with money, much more than the average teenager asking for gas money—as a youngster, he had a fascination with the idea that by investing his money, it could automatically grow year after year. It shouldn't have surprised anyone, then, when he bought his very first mutual fund at the age of *fourteen*. In his words ...

* * *

It was just a normal day at school—until I overheard a conversation that changed my life. Two parents were talking about how anyone can buy stocks and have their money grow larger and larger each year. Some people even became millionaires in the market! Bursting with excitement, I ran home and told my dad that I wanted to invest in the market. I wanted to make millions! I was delighted when he offered to match my $1,500, and together we researched available funds. With his guidance, I found what I thought was a winner. I invested, watched my money grow over the next five years, and sold at a decent profit.

I was hooked.

Like many people, I bounced from one stock to the next, using one strategy after another like a Las Vegas gambler looking for the big win. I was convinced I'd found my ticket to riches: Warren Buffett. His stock-investment method was simple: He invested in consumer monopolies, or what he called "toll bridges". He did the research, then bought accordingly. He looked for stocks that were undervalued and held on to them forever—unless the fundamentals of the company changed.

Sounded like a winner to me, so I switched my investing strategy and started buying large blue chip companies like Coca Cola, McDonald's, and Colgate. For another five years, I did really great.

You can probably guess what happened next.

The stock market crashed.

And because the stock market is no respecter of persons, I—along with everyone else—lost a huge percent of my portfolio in that crash. My dream of watching my dollars multiply had turned into a nightmare.

Notable Wall Street Crashes and Recoveries

1901-03
- Fall in the Dow: 46%
- Losses recovered by July 1905
- 2 years to recover

1906-07
- Fall in the Dow: 49%
- Losses recovered by September 1916
- 9 years to recover

1916-17
- Fall in the Dow: 40%
- Losses recovered by November 1919
- 2 years to recover

1919-21
- Fall in the Dow: 47%
- Losses recovered by November 1924
- 3 years to recover

1929-32
- Fall in the Dow: 89%
- Losses recovered by November 1954
- 22 years to recover

1939-42
- Fall in the Dow: 40%
- Losses recovered by January 1945
- 3 years to recover

1973-74
- Fall in the Dow: 45%
- Losses recovered by December 1982
- 8 years to recover

2008-09
- Fall in the Dow: 48%
- Losses recovered by January 2013
- 5 years to recover

You may have experienced the sickening, desperate feeling of watching your money evaporate right before your eyes with nothing you can do about it!

My Crushing Break-up with Mr. Market

If you've ever seen a relationship start with a deception or lie, you'll know that it usually doesn't turn out too well. No matter the initial strength of the romance, the deception or lie will cause one party to lose all trust for the other partner.

I lost my trust in Mr. Market when this happened to me. I still have moments when I think about the potential to make money buying and selling stocks again. But I quickly come back to reality when I think about losing another decade of wealth.

I realized that continuing to invest directly in the stock market held no guarantees. I had a goal for growing wealthy, and this wasn't helping me reach that goal. All my savings were in the stock market, and I had no control over how that market performed. In fact, there was a very real risk that I could lose *all my money*.

Can You Afford to Lose Another Decade of Wealth?

In May 2010, the Dow Jones Industrial Average was hovering at the same level it did 10 years before. Trillions of dollars were lost in stocks, mutual funds, 401(k)s and other qualified plans. Mr. Market can be extremely rewarding during certain periods, but viciously brutal during others. Dreams are crushed, retirements dashed, and plans delayed. Can you really afford to keep rebuilding your wealth every 5 or 10 years?

The Wall Street Casino

I live close to Vegas and often take trips down with my family. I am always amazed at the luxurious casinos being built. I hear myself saying, "They can't afford to build these huge casinos by paying out winnings to all the customers."

Most people know the house usually wins, yet thousands of people make the trip and continue gambling away their money.

Sadly, many follow the same pattern regarding their wealth—put it at risk in the stock market, hoping for that *one* upward swing that will make them extremely wealthy.

I'm sure that if someone asked you about taking all their retirement money and gambling it on a roulette wheel, you'd instinctively tell him that's probably not a good idea. Yet that's similar to what people do in the market every day. It's the difference between the foolish man who built his house upon the sand of risk and the rich man who built his house on the rock of Safe Money. The tide came in and destroyed the man's house on the sand. The man's house on the rock survived and remained standing strong.

This is exactly why you must PROTECT the PRINCIPAL at all costs.

Take, for example, a $100,000 investment. Assume the market drops by 30% and your money goes from $100,000 to $70,000. How much growth do you need just to get back to even? (Hint: it's not 30%.) You'll actually need 42.5% growth on your money to get back to where you started. Now how long does it take to see a 30% loss in the market? It could happen in as little as one year.

According to the DALBAR Report

"Based on an analysis of actual investor behavior over the 20 years ending December 31, 2011, the average equity investor would have earned an annualized return of 3.49% underperforming the S&P by more than 4.3% and outpacing inflation by a mere 0.49%."

Quantitative Analysis of Investor Behavior (QAIB)

And how long does it take to make your money back? Usually it's not so quick. Let's take a look at some examples in history. [11] After the Great Depression, from 1929-32, the Dow fell 89% and took a full 22 years to recover, Now, 22 years until recovery is a bit dramatic, so let's look at a few more recent drops.

In 1973-74, the Dow fell by approximately 45%. The losses weren't recovered until December 1982. That means a full 8 years could have passed without folks getting any return on their money.

And, of course, most recently the crash of 2008. After the market peaked on October 9, 2007, stocks slid downward. By March 5, 2009, the S&P was down 56% and the Dow down 53%. It took over four years to earn back its losses.

Wall Street seems to have convinced many people that it's necessary to forgo safe, guaranteed returns and risk principal in favor of *possible* 8, 10 or even 12% return on their investments.

Wall Street's favorite tool could be considered a financial calculator showing how much money we'll have in retirement if our money grows at 12 or even 15%!

But often those illustrations leave out several major factors, like market downturns, taxes, and fees.

Unfortunately, due to recent events, we know all too well that even after all the worry, investigation, and research, the gains we've had in our retirement—even after years of growth—can be wiped out with a market downturn.

In just one year during the great recession of 2008, the Dow Jones Industrial lost 1/3 of its value!

There were more than a few Americans who saw their retirement dreams destroyed right before their eyes as their nest egg dropped like a rock. They were powerless to do anything about it.

Another flaw in much of this Wall Street conventional wisdom is that the market actually could provide you a 12-15% return in the first place. DALBAR Inc. (the nation's leading financial services market research firm) shows that the average investor outpaced inflation by just 0.49% over the past several years.

But that's not the story we hear coming out of Wall Street. We often hear about great rates of return. People love to talk about a new hot stock or the latest news on a new tech company that could give them a great rate of return. But let's take a closer look.

> "In a 2012 report on 401(k) fees, the Government Accountability Office (GAO) concluded that such charges (fees) could "significantly decrease retirement savings."
>
> *Government Accountability Office; www.gao.gov*

In our example, Joe starts with $10,000 and gets a 100% rate of return in year one, bouncing his balance up to $20,000.

The next year, the market drops by 50%, leaving him with $10,000 again. In year three, it goes up again by 100% to $20,000, then drops again in the fourth year by 50%, setting him right back at $10,000.

Year	Market	Starting Balance	Ending Balance
1	+ 100%	10,000	20,000
2	- 50%	20,000	10,000
3	+ 100%	10,000	20,000
4	- 50%	20,000	10,000

In this case, the market did average a 25% rate of return. But how much additional cash does Joe have left to show for his 25% average rate of return?

Zero.

Even though brokers quote stats about great rates of return in the market, investors could still be netting absolutely zero.

Take that same $10,000, compound it for four years at 6.5% with no risk in the market, and you could end up with $12,960.20.

A 25% return in the market gave Joe $10,000, but a much lower 6.5% rate, compounded every year, would give him almost $13,000. It's easy to see why people are getting confused about where they should put their money.

Rub Some Salt in the Wound

It's not just market dips that can kill your principal. There are also fees. Often, 401(k)s, mutual funds, and other stock-market-related investments come with fees—fees many people don't understand because they can be very confusing and buried in the fine print.

Compounded over time, this 1-3% fee structure can mean the difference between a comfortable retirement and having to watch every penny. Even if you do realize a 10% return in the market, it could end up being 7-8% after fees.

Even a 1% point difference in fees can have a big impact. Let's take a 35-year-old worker who leaves $20,000 in his 401(k) plan when he switches jobs and never adds to that account. If the account earned 7% a year, minus 0.5% in annual fees, his balance would only grow to about $132,000 at retirement. But if the fees were 1.5% annually, the average net return would be reduced to 5.5%, and the $20,000 would grow to about $100,000. Over 30 years, the 1% increase in fees whittled down the account balance by nearly 25%. [12] Even worse, when you tack on fees while you are losing money, it can be very difficult to regain the ground you've lost so you can start making progress again.

You Can't Grow Your Money If It's Shrinking

When I went back to the drawing board for the last time, I didn't listen to what everyone else was doing. I made a list of what *I* needed. I needed a way to save my money and build financial independence that was simple, easy to follow, and secure—a way that *guaranteed* growth. But that's not all. It also needed to provide good tax benefits, because taxes can ravage your wealth if you aren't careful.

Oh, and wait—I needed to be able to access my money at any time, without getting clobbered by fees and penalties like you would with 401(k) or IRA qualified plans.

I'm happy to say, I found the perfect plan. It's not a get-rich-quick scheme, and it's not gambling with my future. I'm not the only one who's had a bad experience in the market. In fact, many people have been fleeing Wall Street looking for a safer alternative. But many don't know where to look. They are fearful of making a wrong decision and losing even more.

The Wrap

When you start down the Safe Money path, you'll give yourself permission—permission to toss out the old idea that the only way to become wealthy is to risk your hard-earned money, permission to grow wealthy while protecting against some of the other enemies of wealth.

There is good news. There is a solution. The pathway of Safe Money is simple and proven. Soon you will have a clear plan to replace the conventional wisdom that has failed many people, with a proven solution that can give you relief, hope and faith in your future. (In fact, you can grab your own personalized Safe Money blueprint on www.safemoneyretirementbook.com)

With this book, you will now have the blueprint you need to make the moves that can protect your life, family, and finances by creating a rock on which you can build a financial foundation that you can count on.

Section 2

SAFE: Accepting the New Reality

"I must create a system, or be enslaved by another man's."
— William Blake

"Reasonable people adapt themselves to the world.
Unreasonable people attempt to adapt the world to themselves.
All progress, therefore, depends on unreasonable people."
— George Bernard Shaw

Chapter 3

Microwave Money and Pop Culture Gurus

"There are as many opinions as there are experts."
— Franklin D. Roosevelt

"Even when the experts all agree, they may well be mistaken."
— Bertrand Russell

"Bear Stearns is not in trouble!"

"I believe in the Bear Stearns Franchise. At 69 bucks, I'm not giving up on the thing!"

These statements were both made by Jim Cramer of *Mad Money* CNBC, uttered on March 6th and March 11th, 2008. 11 days later, Bear Sterns stock had dropped from $69.00 to $2.00.

Who controls the financial education most people get these days? Think for a second about who most people are listening to. You may have read articles from pop culture money magazines. You might have followed the popular TV personalities or read their books. You may have listened to the HR department at work suggesting you invest in the 401(k) because you'll get matching funds. Free money!

Wait just a minute. Did you know that the 401(k) and other qualified retirement programs are trillion-dollar businesses? By some estimates, there are between 7 and 11 trillion dollars in qualified plans. That's a lot of money to trust to Wall Street stockbrokers and their computer systems. Could it be possible that there is a little self-interest going on? Might it be that investment bankers, stockbrokers, and brokerage houses are *keenly* interested in selling that Wall Street conventional wisdom because that's how they make a living?

Do They Practice What They Preach?

Almost everybody's heard of—if not listened to—Suze Orman, the personal finance expert. Orman hosts her own show, has written a handful of bestsellers, and was named by *Time* magazine as one of the world's one hundred most influential people. She encourages viewers, listeners, and readers to buy term and invest (remember: investing = risking) the difference in mutual funds.

But does she practice what she preaches?

She estimates her liquid net worth at about $25 million, with an additional $7 million in houses. Where is the majority of her money invested?

"I save it and build it in municipal bonds. I buy zero-coupon municipal bonds and all the bonds I buy are triple-A-rated, and insured so even if the city goes under, I get my money," Orman says.

Doesn't sound like *she's* risking her money in the market, does it? That's a safe money strategy if I've ever heard one.

When asked about playing the stock market, she says that, "I have a million dollars in the stock market, because if I lose a million dollars, I don't personally care." In short, the financial guru coaching the American public has a portfolio few ever will.

Maybe someone who can afford to lose $1 million has no qualms about encouraging other people to invest in the market too.

Of course, it probably doesn't hurt that one of her personal sponsors is TD Ameritrade. TD Ameritrade is a huge company that makes money facilitating stock trades. Suze Orman is often seen on advertisements encouraging people to open up an account with TD Ameritrade. Now, does Orman's advice to buy term and invest the difference in the market sound fishy to you?

Then of course there's Jim Cramer, investment guru and host of CNBC's *Mad Money*, who advises that people invest their mad money—or in other words, non-retirement funds—in the stock market. Cramer regularly makes recommendations not only to his own show's viewers, but to audiences of NBC's *Today Show*, steering people to the market buys he thinks will pay off handsomely.

How's That Been Working?

Not so well, according to news reports. As one example, reported by the *Wall Street Cheat Sheet,* Cramer recommended that viewers buy CIT Group, a stock he said that was primed for upside. Fewer than four weeks later, CIT filed bankruptcy. The *Cheat Sheet's* assessment? "This type of incredibly speculative advice is as radioactive to the general investing public as a post nuclear explosion site... If "In Cramer You Trust", (like the CNBC commercials tell you to do), you are probably going to have lost over 90% of your investment by the open on Monday." [13]

Summing it all up, a report in *Baron's* stated that, "Cramer is wildly inconsistent, and the performance of individual picks varies widely. So widely, in fact, that it is impossible to know with confidence that any sample of Cramer's recommendations will enable you to outperform the market." [14]

These are just two examples of the media promoting the Wall Street conventional wisdom that has a questionable (at best) track record of success and often proves just the opposite! In fact, they've done such a good job convincing Americans of the conventional financial wisdom of investing in stock, maxing out 401(k)s, buying term and then investing the difference, that we've seen millions of people lose trillions of dollars by following each other like sheep right off the financial cliff. [15]

Our Safe Money paths have people build their house on a solid foundation. Contractors don't put buildings on foundations of clay or sand. They use concrete. Why, then, would we be any less careful with our entire financial future? The solid foundation we are talking about is Safe

Money. It's the safety net you can count on in good times and bad. Our Safe Money paths allow us not to worry about the market roller coaster. We grow our foundations without risk, and plus, we have many other living benefits. We'll get to those shortly.

The Wrap

So far on our Safe Money path, we've covered three critical topics:

1. Wall Street conventional financial wisdom has failed many Americans. It's time to leave the status quo behind.

2. Investing in the market holds no guarantees. It is more like building your financial house on a foundation of sand.

3. Pop culture financial gurus get paid to fill air time, not make you wealthy. In fact, following their advice can cost you big time.

But the fun doesn't end there. There's another force we have to contend with. An extraordinary story about a bank robber named Willie Sutton might shed some light on it for you.

CHAPTER 4

THE WILLIE SUTTON SLAP DOWN

*"In this world nothing can be said to be certain,
except death and taxes."*
— Benjamin Franklin

Willie Sutton wasn't born a bank robber.

Willie was the fourth of five children born to an ordinary Brooklyn family on June 30, 1901. Like all the other kids in Brooklyn, he went to school. But he didn't stick with it very long. Filled with dreams, he left home after the eighth grade in search of fame and fortune.

But Willie had a problem. He loved expensive clothes and the finer things of life—things that were hard to finance on the meager wages he brought in from his string of menial jobs like gardening, clerking, and drilling. Never satisfied, he jumped from one job to another with alarming frequency. His longest period of continuous employment was 18 months.

At the age of 28, he got married. But his wedded bliss was short-lived because his wife divorced him when he landed in jail. You see, Willie Sutton had finally found a career that offered fatter paychecks, albeit riskier working conditions. Willie Sutton was a bank robber.

After serving a brief stint, Willie was back on the streets and back at his lucrative profession. According to the FBI, Willie Sutton mastered the art of disguise—a talent that earned him the nickname "The Actor". He attempted to rob the Corn Exchange Bank and Trust Company in Philadelphia, Pennsylvania, disguised as a mailman. The curiosity of a passerby derailed his plans. (Not to worry: he returned to the same bank less than a year later and this time was successful.) At other times, he disguised himself as a messenger, policeman, or maintenance man. He pulled off a sizable heist at a Broadway jewelry store in broad daylight by disguising himself as a telegraph messenger.

In addition to his innovative disguises, Willie was distinguished from other bank robbers by his gentle demeanor. Victims of his robberies and innocent bystanders in the teller lines reported how polite he was. Many commented that he behaved like a real gentleman. One victim quipped that witnessing a Willie Sutton robbery was like being at the movies, except the usher had a gun.

In June 1931, Willie's luck ran out—sort of. He was charged with assault and robbery, found guilty, and sentenced to 30 years in prison. But again, that 18-month charm kicked in. 18 months after he was incarcerated, just in time to celebrate Christmas in 1932, Willie roped two nine-foot sections of ladder together and scaled up and over the prison wall.

On February 5, 1934, Willie returned to the Corn Exchange Bank and Trust Company—this time with a machine gun. Things didn't go so well. He was apprehended and sentenced to serve 25 to 50 years in the Eastern State Penitentiary in Philadelphia.

Fast-forward a year to April 3, 1945. Willie Sutton was one of 12 convicts who burrowed out of the penitentiary through a tunnel—his *fifth* escape attempt from the same prison. Philadelphia police officers recaptured him the same day. He was tossed back in prison, this time for life as a fourth-time offender. Just to be on the safe side, officials transferred him to the Philadelphia County Prison in Holmesburg, Pennsylvania—away from the prison where he'd practiced so many escapes.

Willie lasted almost two years at Holmesburg before he and a group of other prisoners dressed up as prison guards, sashayed across the prison yard after dark, and carried two ladders to the prison wall. Caught in the beams of the prison searchlight, Willie Sutton flashed a grin and yelled, "It's okay," and kept moving with his plan. No one stopped him. He was free again.

On March 20, 1950, a little more than three years after he walked away from Holmesburg, Willie Sutton was added to the FBI list of Ten Most Wanted Fugitives. In addition to distributing his poster to police departments throughout the nation, the FBI also gave his photograph to tailors. After all, this was a man who dressed impeccably in expensive, tailored clothing. Two years later, Willie was nonchalantly riding a New York City subway when a twenty-four-year-old tailor's son recognized him as the man from the wanted posters. He quietly followed Willie to a gas station and watched him buy a battery for his car before he called the police with the tip.

Face-to-face with New York's finest, Willie Sutton didn't resist arrest. But he also didn't fess up to any robberies— or any other crimes, for that matter. He was hauled into Queens County Court, where he was sentenced to an additional 30 years to life. It was a drop in the bucket. Willie already owed one life sentence plus 105 years. They tossed him into a cell at Attica State Prison and threw away the key. If all went according to plan, he'd never see daylight again.

Of course, that wasn't the end of the story. Seventeen years later, the system took pity on Willie. He was seriously ill with emphysema and needed major surgery on the arteries in both his legs. On Christmas Eve of 1969, the State of New York released Willie Sutton from prison. He was sixty-eight. Just two years later in an irony that's stranger than fiction, Willie did a television commercial to promote the new photo credit card for—what else?—a Connecticut bank.

Willie Sutton died November 2, 1980, in Florida at the age of seventy-nine. Before he died, he authored two books about his illustrious career as a bank robber. And when asked why he robbed banks, he smiled and simply replied, "Because that's where the money is." [16]

Willie Sutton's Law

Why did Willie rob banks? Willie said it best himself: he robbed banks because that's where the money was.

Wherever wealth is accumulated, someone will always try to take it. In some circles, this type of human behavior is called "Willie Sutton's Law".

If you are like most Americans, you may feel you are living Willie Sutton's Law every day. Shallow bank balances, high expenses, credit card statements, and bills on the counter make us feel as though someone is constantly trying to take our money away!

But before you sell the car, cut up the credit cards, and stop buying food for the dog, let's take a better look at exactly who might be trying to rob you. The following tactics are completely legal, and unless you are aware, you might not even see them coming.

Who is the modern-day Willie Sutton imposter? It is the Tax Man.

But wait! Shouldn't we all share the cost of doing business in this country by sharing the costs of education, paving roads, and running the government? Sure—that was the idea. But if you're not careful, and if you blindly follow the Wall Street conventional wisdom by investing in qualified retirement plans, you may one day have a sickening scene unfold in front of you. You could end up losing a massive chunk of your retirement to taxes, much more than you bargained for. There's a legal and ethical way to prevent that, and you'll be excited when you see how simple it is to accomplish.

Under the Tax Man's Thumb

You are probably aware that, depending on your tax bracket, the Tax Man could be grabbing up to 20-30% of your paycheck every pay period. (Did you know that

Thomas Jefferson said that an income tax of even 1% is equivalent to slavery?) Wait a minute. Wasn't it you that commuted in rush-hour traffic, dealt with upset customers, and missed out on the kids' baseball games while working those 50+ hour weeks? You do the all work, yet the Tax Man always takes his cut.

But income tax is just the beginning—the proverbial tip of the iceberg. Take a second and think of all the other taxes you might be paying: state income tax, social security tax, property tax, Medicare tax, phone tax, utility tax, sales tax, gasoline tax, and vehicle tax—not just on the purchase, but also on the annual registration. And in the next few years, we could be looking at unprecedented levels of healthcare taxes. [17] In fact, almost every transaction you make is taxed.

Consider your average morning. Almost every time you brush your teeth, turn on a light, eat a bowl of cereal, use the phone, or access the Internet, taxes take a bite.

When you get in your car, drive down the road, go out to lunch, or even take out the trash, the Tax Man is right there in the shadows, like Willie Sutton, to take your money. It's enough to drive you crazy. So doesn't it seem sheer lunacy, then, to pay even more taxes on the money you save for retirement?

The Trillion-dollar Tax Target

Hey, wait a minute! Hasn't the government established tax-deferred programs to help people save and invest for retirement *without* paying taxes up front? Indeed, but remember Willy Sutton's Law? Wherever wealth is accumulated, someone will be there to steal it.

Do you have any idea how much wealth is accumulated in government-sponsored qualified retirement plans like IRAs and 401(k)s?

Trillions of Dollars

If you aren't careful, the profits of these plans could end up largely being Uncle Sam's. Here's why. Imagine for just a minute that you're a farmer. You purchase a bag of corn seed. As the sun begins to dip below the horizon on that late spring evening, you gaze out over your fields, filled with the anticipation of an abundant harvest following months of sustained labor.

As time goes by, you do everything right. You fertilize, water, weed, tend, and protect. At last comes the time of harvest, and the abundance you imagined is realized ten times over. You're filled with the satisfaction of a job well done as you watch a convoy of trucks taking your crops to market.

As the last trailer disappears from sight, a shiny sedan roars up, tires crunching in the gravel at the edge of the road. Out hops a well-dressed man who looks suspiciously like Willie Sutton. As you remove your hat and wipe your well-worn sleeve across your dampened brow, he opens a notebook and stands with ball-point pen ready. Without so much as an introduction—because, really, he doesn't need one—he poses the question: "So, farmer, you have two options. Do you want to pay taxes on that bag of seed you hauled in here last spring, or on the five trucks of crops you just sent to market?"

He's kidding, right?

No. He's not.

Because as a farmer, you have a choice. You can pay taxes on the seed—the money you start out with—or you can pay taxes on the crop, which represents all the increase that grew from your initial seed money.

In the government-sponsored, tax-deferred retirement plans, you pay taxes on all the increase. You're paying taxes on the truckloads of crops. With the plan we'll show you, you pay taxes on the seed. The crops are yours, and you get to keep all the money you grow.

To help you more clearly understand how this works, let's look at some actual figures.

Option 1: The 7702 Plan™

Invest $5,000 a year for 30 years.

Total of $150,000.

In a 33% tax bracket, you pay $49,500 in taxes on that money as you earn it over the 30 years.

Assume you experience a 6.5% growth rate on that money. By the end of the 30 years, you'll have $348,854.18 in your account.

(Get your own personalized 7702 Plan ™ on
www.safemoneyretirementbook.com)

Option 2: A tax-deferred plan like a 401(k)

Invest $5,000 a year in the stock market for 30 years.

Growth rate: 6.5%

Total of $498,017.98.

You didn't pay taxes up front on this money, so you've

now got more money. Okay, you're probably thinking, this is a no brainer—I'll take the tax-deferred plan with the bigger balance!

But wait—remember Willie Sutton? He's clicking his ball-point pen. How much of that $498,017.98 belongs to Uncle Sam? You have $498,017.98 in your retirement account. Let's say you take out $73,000 a year to live on during retirement. You can take $73,000 a year out of your account for nine years before your money is gone (assuming it's still growing at 6.5%). On that $73,000 each year, you now have to pay taxes on the "crop" (assuming you are in the same 33% tax bracket). Thus, you will pay $24,090 in taxes every year. In nine years, you will have paid $216,810 in taxes.

Remember how much you saved by deferring taxes— by waiting to pay on the crop instead of on the seed? You saved $49,500. That means you will have paid Uncle Sam back everything you saved in just the first two and a half years. In the next six and a half years, you will pay an additional $167,310 in taxes on your harvest.

In fact, according to Scott Shultz, you could end up paying up to five times more taxes using a qualified plan like a 401(k) than you saved during your entire working years. [18]

Now ask yourself that question again: Would I rather pay taxes on my seed or on my crop?

Conventional wisdom says you'll be in a lower tax bracket when you retire, so deferring taxes is a good thing. Not so fast. In later years, people often lose many of the deductions they presently have because kids have moved out and mortgages have been paid off.

Plus, do you know what the tax rates are going to be when you retire? How does the federal government plan to pay back the trillion-dollar deficit? None of us, not even the most seasoned prognosticator, can predict where taxes will be when you retire. But a quick look back into history shows tax brackets that have been as high as 92%.

The good news is that you don't have to pay on your crop. We'll show you how to beat old Willie Sutton by paying on your seed so you can enjoy your full harvest. By paying on your seed, you are still meeting your tax obligation. This difference is, you're just not over-paying.

Paying tax on the seed gives you major tax advantages on your growth, while at the same time protecting the principal from risks in the market. You can have access to your money throughout your life (even if that's next month or next year or all the way into your retirement). It also allows you to transfer your wealth to your heirs without them having to pay income tax on that money.

The Wrap

The Safe Money path is not just about keeping your money safe from market losses. It's about protecting your money from all the enemies of wealth, like taxes, market losses, and brokerage fees. But it doesn't end there. It gives you another arrow in your arsenal to defeat another foe: the interest vampire.

CHAPTER 5

KILLING THE
INTEREST VAMPIRE

*"There are two types of people in the world.
Those who pay interest and those who EARN it."*
— Unknown

*"The rich rule over the poor,
and the borrower is servant to the lender."*
— Proverbs 22:7

*"Banks don't lend their money.
They lend the money somebody else left there."*
— Adam Smith

I was shocked when I awoke from my zombie-like state.

Much like yours, my day was pretty routine. I woke up, went to work, came home, saw the family, ate dinner, went to sleep, and did it all over again the next morning. Every two weeks, the paycheck came in and immediately disappeared, going to mortgage payments, car payments, credit card payments, and other expenses.

At the end of the month, I had worked hard, but had little to show for it. I was a member of the financial living dead, going through the motions to pay everyone else, but not myself.

Like most Americans, I was having the financial life sucked right out of me by the vampire of interest.

How would you like a 34% raise? Of course you would.

If you're an average American, you could be paying a whopping 34% of your after-tax income in interest. [19]

Take out a twenty from your wallet, rip a 1/3 of it off, and that's about how much of your after-tax income could be going to interest every year.

You might be saying to yourself, "I shop really hard for good interest rates. I check not only the price of what I'm buying, but I also work hard to keep my credit score high so I can get a good interest rate on my purchases."

Price and interest rate are the two factors everyone focuses on—but they're not the things that kill you. The killer is the *volume* of interest.

Imagine you go buy a car for $30,000 and get a five-year loan with an interest rate of 7.5%. How much will you pay in interest over the life of that

Safe Money Alert

Your 7.5% car loan could end up costing you more like 20.2% by the time you pay off that loan!

loan? Easy, you say, whipping out your calculator: 7.5% of $30,000 is $2,250.

Right?

Wrong! You'll actually pay more than twice that much. The amount of interest you will pay on that $30,000 car loan could be up to $6,068.31—20.2% of the amount you borrowed.

Wait! How is that possible?

It happens because of three letters that follow your interest rate quote: APR, or annual percentage rate. The 7.5% is the rate you pay on the balance of the loan every year. So by the time you are done paying off your car loan, you'll have paid over 20% on that loan, not just 7.5%!

Here's where the volume of interest comes in. Let's say, over the course of your lifetime, you finance 10 cars at $30,000 each. That's a total of $300,000. Assuming you get the same 7.5% interest on those loans, that means you'll pay about $6,000 in interest on each loan, or $60,000 in interest on your 10 cars. I don't know about you, but I think $60,000 is a big deal. A really big deal—especially when current figures reveal that the average American reaches retirement age with only $88,000 in savings. That means you will have dumped out, in interest

> **Safe Money Alert**
>
> If you thought interest on cars was hard to swallow, this might really make you sick. Home loans are front-loaded with most of the interest paid in the first years of the loan. Because of how often people refinance homes, over 10 or 20 years of paying down mortgages, up to 86% of every dollar you pay on your mortgage could be going straight to interest!

on cars, almost as much as most people save for their entire retirement. (We won't even cover leasing here. Leasing cars can often turn out to be even worse than traditional financing.)

With purchase price and interest combined on your 10 cars, even if you keep them until they're paid off, you will have kissed away $360,000 on your cars. We're talking a total of *four times* what many people save for their retirement.

What if you could keep the majority of that $360,000 flowing back into YOUR pocket instead of some lender or car company?

You can.

To introduce you to this great financial tool, I want to tell you about one of my favorite movies, *Déjà Vu*, starring Denzel Washington.

At one point in the movie, Denzel faced an impossible task. He had to explain to the woman he was trying to save that he was from the future. (Try coming up with a good explanation for that one!) It was vital to her survival that she know what was happening, so he asked her this critical question: "What if you had to tell someone the most important thing in the world, but you knew they wouldn't believe you?"

After thinking for a moment, she looked at him and thoughtfully replied, "I'd still try."

So now it's our turn to ask you a critical question: What if you could help people solve some of their biggest financial problems, but you were afraid no one would believe you?

Hopefully you'd reply, "I'd still try."

50

There are many people who would prefer that you not discover this incredible financial tool. In fact, some gurus actively discredit it as too ineffective or antiquated, but you and I both know better than to believe everything they say. Banks, stockbrokers, mutual fund managers, and most gurus never promote it.

Why? Because it doesn't serve them—it serves you.

Financing Your Own Prosperity™

You've seen how the system has been set up to make a few people rich while giving the average person more financial frustration. But by using a time-tested financial tool we call a 7702 Plan™, you can set yourself up to enjoy the cars, home improvement projects, and vacations you want—without paying interest to a bank or credit card company. Plus, you get to recoup your principal and put it back into your plan rather than lose it forever on whatever you are buying.

Here's how Financing Your Own Prosperity™ works:

1. First, you accumulate cash value into a 7702 Plan™.

2. When you are ready to buy your next car, go on vacation, or make any other major purchase, you borrow against your cash value. No credit check, no applications, no getting declined. Now you can make that purchase with cash.

3. Lastly, instead of paying a bank or credit card company, you pay yourself back. If you choose to pay extra interest, it will only increase your own cash value.

The Really Exciting Part

When you Finance Your Own Prosperity™ with a 7702 Plan™, the cash value continues to grow as if you've never touched the money.

That's right. You can take $30,000 out for a new car and your money continues to grow with the same guaranteed rate, as if it was never touched.

I know this sounds too good to be true. I thought the same thing when I learned about it. But don't worry. I'll show you exactly how this happens in just a minute.

The 7702 Plan™ is simple, secure, and guaranteed. It's built using a special type of cash value life insurance policy.

I can already hear you saying, "Life insurance? Are you serious?"

Now before you jump ship because you hate life insurance, let me tell you—I was one of you. I never believed in cash value life insurance because for years I had bought into the "buy term and invest the difference" hype from gurus.

We've already covered why investing the difference may not work out very well—primarily because of taxes, fees, and market dips. Not to mention many people simply don't have the discipline to actually invest the difference—it just gets spent!

Some people don't like cash value insurance because they've heard from pop culture gurus (enter Suze Orman and Dave Ramsey) that it's not a good investment. That's why it's important to use a 7702 Plan™, a modified cash value life insurance policy that allows you to grow the cash value as quickly as possible (in some cases up to 3-5 times faster than traditional life insurance policies), while putting as little money as possible toward insurance costs.

The Wrap

Take a look at some of the benefits that a 7702 Plan™ could offer:

- Safe, guaranteed growth every year

- A time-tested financial product that has been stable for more than 100 years

- Largely untouched by major market crashes

- Guaranteed growth and principal

- Tax-advantaged growth (You can access your money without a taxable event!)

- Flexible financial tool allowing you to access money for major purchases, college funding, or other needs. (And most importantly for this chapter, it could allow you to Finance Your Own Prosperity™.)

Now that you understand the benefits a 7702 Plan™ could bring, let's see them in action.

SECTION 3

SAFE: BUILDING A SAFE MONEY FOUNDATION

"Do you wish to rise?
Begin by descending.
You plan a tower that will pierce the clouds?
Lay first the foundation."

— St. Augustine

CHAPTER 6

DEFEATING THE ENEMIES OF WEALTH

"Wherever wealth is accumulated,
someone will be there to try and steal it."
— R. Nelson Nash

Jason Smith slid into the front seat, slammed the door, and slumped forward until his forehead pressed against the steering wheel. His stomach was in knots and a dull ache throbbed behind his temples. Another roller coaster week in the market had dropped his 401(k) value substantially.

He dreaded facing Susan. After all, it had been *his* idea to max out the 401(k). She'd wanted to keep their contributions smaller—to put some of Jason's salary in a conventional savings account or maybe some short-term CDs. She worried about emergencies and about covering the kids' college expenses—all arguments that he disregarded at the time.

He'd read some articles written by the industry's top gurus, and he figured he knew what he was doing. He knew that the 401(k) was the most popular retirement plan in America. He not only wanted all the free money he could get through his employer's match, but he'd heard about the great tax savings to be had from socking the maximum amount possible into a 401(k). All the other guys in his department were doing it and they seemed savvy enough.

Jason had won out, and for the past six years a large percentage of every paycheck had gone to his 401(k) account. It had seemed like a good idea at the time. But that was *before*.

Before the market experienced a nearly unprecedented crash that slashed the value of mutual funds and crushed retirement accounts of people all over the country.

Before he'd found out—how had he not known this?— that the money in his 401(k) might as well have been locked up in Fort Knox because it was a major pain to get at any of it. After all, it was *his* money. And he needed some of it. And now—easing reluctantly up the driveway—Jason knew that what had seemed like such a good idea six years ago was turning out to be an emotional and financial roller coaster with more downs than ups.

Jason sank onto the sofa in the living room and proceeded to tell Susan the bad news. Another drop in economic forecasts had caused a major drop in the market, which was costing them thousands with every drop. First off, his account was not even worth *half* of what he thought it was. His hard-earned money was gone, thanks to the plunge of a market over which he had no control.

So much for his plan of retiring with millions like he'd dreamed about.

Second, Susan had really wanted to access some money for the kitchen remodel they badly needed. If he took the money out, he'd be slapped with so many fees and penalties—including an enormous tax penalty—that he'd scarcely even break even.

Even if he decided to brave the penalties, he'd lose a fortune selling the funds in his account when the market was so low. He would kiss away what hadn't already been lost to the market crash.

Finally, he didn't even dare borrow from his account. The little carrot that had been dangled in front of his nose six years ago turned out to have a very painful string attached.

What they hadn't told Jason when he invested in a 401(k) was that if he lost his job, the loan would be due in full, usually within two months' time.

With a rumored corporate merger in the works that could result in potential layoffs, that was a chance Jason couldn't afford to take.

Maxing out the 401(k)—not the best idea, Jason sheepishly admitted.

A few days later, after some emails between friends, Jason got a link to an online site that could compute his True Financial Age. He was intrigued.

It would tell him his "Never Work Again" number. He started punching in numbers, thinking things couldn't possibly get worse, and while he was a bit shocked at what he saw, he also got some good news.

Jason Smith, at age 42, had a True Financial Age of 81.

Simply put, here's what that means: In order to have enough money put away for retirement, Jason would have to work until he was 81 years old.

Eighty-one? Jason wasn't sure he'd even *live* that long! As visions of greeting customers at the local warehouse store clouded his thoughts, he noticed that the website offered a way out—and it could all be explained by a Safe Money Associate. ™ Let's just say it was a hard sell for Susan. We can imagine why she might be just a little skeptical about Jason's financial know-how right about now.

Reluctantly, Susan agreed, and Jason filled out the request online to meet with an SMA, Michael, who said he could help them get on the Safe Money path while kissing the stock market roller coaster good-bye.

It was done using a 100-year-old proven way to keep your money safe. It came with guaranteed growth each year, a way to potentially experience the ups of the markets without the downs . . . and could give you the ability to access your cash value throughout your life. In fact, that was one of the major benefits of the plan—that you could use it to Finance Your Own Prosperity™. This meant you could borrow against your plan for major purchases like cars, college tuition, or vacations and then pay your loan back to yourself while the cash continued to grow as if you hadn't touched it. Jason was particularly intrigued by that idea. Ultimately, it was a way to possibly reduce the amount of interest you would pay to banks or credit card companies!

Let's take a break in the story while we're waiting for Michael to show up and get a few of the basics out of the way. Because whether you have a 401(k) or not, this will be a new information. And like GI Joe says, "Knowing is half the battle."

You might have assumed, just like our friend Jason, that a 401(k) or mutual fund is a solid way to save for retirement. After all, that's what many of the pop culture gurus advocate. Right out of the gate, let's see what one financial analyst had to say about it:

The American public has been hoodwinked by political and corporate forces into relying on the 401(k) as the primary long-term investment mechanism. In doing so, the stock market has been put at center stage in providing for a comfortable retirement for the average American. The 401(k) represents an implicit promise to middle-class Americans that they can live off the income that they receive from stock ownership, just like the rich do. It is a promise impossible to fulfill; it is the great 401(k) hoax. [20]

"Hoax" sounds like a pretty strong word, but that's potentially what the 401(k) plan is.

Here's a quick crash course on 401(k) plans. Money in 401(k) plans is often invested in stocks and mutual funds. If the market goes up, so can your money. If you have money in a 401 (k) with stocks or mutual funds, your money could be at risk for loss!

That means if the market goes down, you can lose. Lastly, your 401(k) contributions are made *before* you pay taxes on the money, so you're taxed as you withdraw money from the plan. (Here's where you see that you are being taxed on the crop, not the seed.) And don't forget, your money could be tied up until you retire, unless you want to pay the penalties and taxes on an early withdrawal.

Now, let's get back to the meeting with Michael.

It's seven o'clock on Thursday evening, and Michael, Jason, and Susan are sitting around the kitchen table. Jason is all ears. But Susan, feeling like she's just had the proverbial blanket yanked out from under her feet with the 401(k) debacle, is hanging back. Susan, still skeptical, goes for the jugular with this comment:

"I need to ask something right up front," she says. Michael welcomes the question. After detailing what had just happened with their 401(k), Susan squares herself up in her chair. "We've listened to other financial gurus and advisors and it's gotten us where we are now. Why should we listen to you?"

"I understand your skepticism in talking with another financial advisor. The difference is, I'm focused on Safe Money. I help people build a strong foundation of safety so they never lose money in the market downturns. 401(k) plans or mutual funds can be the *risky* kind of investing," Michael explains. "In fact, depending on how you direct your contributions, it could put all of your retirement principal at risk." Susan, clearly frustrated, glares at Jason.

"Tonight I'm going to talk to you about some of the biggest enemies of building wealth and also about how you can start on the Safe Money path to retirement.

"A couple of the threats that we must protect against to have a Safe Money retirement are 1) the actual loss of your money in the market (once you lose money, it can take a substantial amount of time to make it up), 2) taxes, and 3) interest. Many folks don't know it, but they could be paying up to one-third of every dollar they make toward interest of some sort. This is essentially making them employees of the tax man and the lenders at the same time.

"Let's talk about putting your money at risk of loss. To begin, let's look at how your mutual fund or stock performs. How much money you end up with for retirement usually depends completely on the market," Michael explains. "The market is uncertain, risky, and completely out of your control. So your future is tied to how well the market cooperates, without any input from you."

While Jason and Susan tried to wrap their heads around that piece of information, Michael started asking some pretty tough questions. "Jason, how much do you really know about your 401(k)?"

"Clearly not as much as I thought I did," Jason mumbles.

"Well, let's start with your 401(k) manager—do you even know who it is?" Jason shakes his head, and Michael goes on. "Do you know what funds you're invested in or even what companies your funds invest in? Most people enrolled in 401(k) plans can't even list the funds or companies in which they are investing. That's risky business."

"Interesting," Susan smugly replies. "That sounds more like *gambling* to me."

"There's more," Michael says. "I know that you've already found out about some of the tax implications. Think about this: If you don't like paying taxes right now, what makes you think you're going to like it any better 20 years from now? When you start to withdraw your 401(k) money for retirement, you're going to have to pay taxes on it. That means if you're in a 28% tax bracket, you could have about one-third less actual money than you have in your account."

(A quick point: in a 401(k) plan, you'll be paying taxes on the crop, not the seed. And this is called tax savings? What an irony. People invest in a 401(k) plan to save taxes, but in reality, they could end up actually paying *more* taxes— not only because they're paying on the crop, but because they could potentially be in a higher tax bracket when they begin taking distributions from their 401(k) plans.)

"You've got three children, right?" Michael asks. Susan nods. "If you don't manage to use up your 401(k) during your retirement, it will be passed on to your heirs. Not only could they face income tax on the money they receive from your 401(k), but they could have to pay estate taxes as well. If you have more than $1 million in your estate, it could amount to 55%.

"There's another issue with a 401(k) plan you need to be aware of—fees. Many folks don't know how much in fees they are really paying. Unfortunately, it can add up to a substantial sum, and the fund managers always get paid whether your money grows or not."

Jason slaps his palm against the table. "I feel like I've been misled. Our HR guy pushed a bunch of papers in front of me and encouraged me to sign on the dotted line, all the while touting matching funds and company support. But he never said anything about getting out! All the gurus on TV, and everyone else for that matter, say to max out my 401(k)."

Susan clears her throat loudly.

"Oh, yeah, well—everyone except Susan," Jason admits.

Now both Jason and Susan are now ready to listen to Michael. He's shown them why the old way wasn't working. Jason feels like he's learned more about the 401(k) program in the last 20 minutes than in the previous two decades.

Susan, who has softened a little toward Jason, says, "I'm feeling ripped off too. Just yesterday, I read a column by a well-respected financial guru. Her advice was to buy term and invest the difference in mutual funds. It's ironic that she was the spokesperson for TD Ameritrade who probably makes millions off people who invest in the market through their system."

How efficient do you think the average business would be if it suffered constant turnover—in other words, if new people came in on a regular basis, bringing new ideas and new ways of doing things? Well, that's what happens with mutual funds—except instead of people, the turnover involves stocks (in other words, excessive trading in the portfolio). Mutual fund managers are constantly changing the stocks in the portfolio. (Translation: you never know from one day to the next exactly *what's* in your portfolio.)

In the 1950s, the average portfolio turnover rate was about 15%. Today, 100% turnover is commonplace, and as much as 300% turnover is typical. Just a few years ago, *Forbes* magazine reported turnover rates so high that even the reporter was astonished. Rates ranged from 523% to a staggering 827%. The result of all these turnovers is that the cost of doing business for mutual funds, instead of going down, has doubled since the 1950s. And who pays for the increased cost? That's right: the investors. Lucky dogs. [21]

Jason chuckles. "Yeah, we've both seen the results of those."

"We all watched as the market toppled," says Michael, "taking with it the retirement dreams of millions of Americans. Even those who had enjoyed growth watched as their nest eggs were crushed to nearly half their previous value. And they were powerless to do anything about it. But you know what?" Michael continues. "Even without the disastrous crash we recently witnessed, there are always ups and downs that we can't control. Studies have shown that over the past 180 years, the average market return after factoring for inflation is as low as 1.2%. [22]

"Here's what it amounts to," Michael says. "As an investor, you put up 100% of the money, and you take 100% of the risk. *You're* the one whose principal is on the line. This is fine if you have money you can stand to lose, but this is *not* the way that Safe Money retirees live. They build a solid foundation and protect the principal. You guys got started on the right foot by visiting our site, www.safemoneyretirementbook.com, right?"

"Yeah, I found your site because a friend referred me to it. I took the Safe Money Quiz, and it was really eye-opening. I felt like it was time to try a different approach."

Susan interjects, "The Safe Money program sounds good to me."

"It does make sense," Jason agrees. "But I'm not sure what to do at this point. I'm stuck in a crummy 401(k) I can't get out of, and I'm not thinking I can afford any mutual funds for a while— at least not until we pull out of the hole we're in. So, what do we do now?"

Michael smiles again and starts spreading out his papers. "Jason, I've got great news for you."

"It's about time I got some *good* news for a change!" Jason laughs.

"You're a whole lot better informed than when I got here," Michael points out. "And now I'm going to show you how you *can* get on the right track, starting today. Regardless of your situation with the 401(k), I think we'll find some good solutions together. I'm going to show you a plan that will keep your money safely out of the market, is guaranteed to grow every year, and offers a smart tax strategy that allows *you* to Finance Your Own Prosperity™. You could reduce or totally eliminate the amount you pay in interest to banks and credit card companies, plus, have access to your cash value throughout your life. It's called the 7702 Plan™. And it's a plan you can start right away. Sound good?"

Jason feels like he's about to cry again—this time from relief.

CHAPTER 7

FINANCE YOUR OWN PROSPERITY™

"All truths are easy to understand once they are discovered;
the point is to discover them."
— Galileo

"In very simple terms," Michael explains, "the 7702 Plan™ is a customized cash value life insurance policy. In the next few minutes, I'm going to show you how it's not only a protection plan, but a powerful Safe Money plan."

"Oh, no!" Susan cries. "Hold on. I've heard both Suze Orman and Dave Ramsey say that it's a bad idea to buy cash value life insurance."

"Yeah," Jason chimes in. "My buddy who's a CPA says cash value life insurance is the wrong way to go. Lots of the financial pieces I've studied paint a poor picture of it too. They say it's just too expensive."

"I'm going to debunk those myths for you in just a few minutes," Michael says, "and you're going to see how cash value life insurance—*if* it's structured properly—can be a very solid solution for building wealth."

"Better than term insurance?" Jason asks.

"It's in a different league than term insurance," Michael says. "Term insurance is important for one reason: to provide for your family in the event of an untimely death. It's a bit like renting, really. You rent the insurance for a set period of years, and after that term of 10 or 20 years is up, your insurance is gone. There's usually no equity in term policies. However, if you do happen to die during those years, your beneficiaries receive the death benefit from your policy."

Michael continues, "We, as Americans, spend more money insuring our cars than we do our lives. In fact, we actually do things in reverse: We focus on protecting the golden eggs—cars, homes, and other possessions—instead of protecting the goose that lays those golden eggs."

"I have to admit I'm guilty of that," Jason murmurs. "Pretty much all I've got is my little policy through work— a term policy—but, man, I sure shell it out on insurance for the cars and the house."

Michael nods in understanding. "A 7702 Plan™, using cash value insurance, can provide death benefit protection like term, but it also provides you with a safe place for your money. It's also sometimes referred to as *permanent* life insurance. And it's just what its name implies, too: it covers you until you die, as long as you keep the policy in force. While we've all watched the stock market rise and fall, with banks and companies failing, the insurance industry has

1. You want an insurance company with a long history of success and financial stability. One of the companies we work with has been in business for over 300 years and actually insured the home that Isaac Newton lived in.

2. You need an advisor who has been trained to create maximum cash value growth without hurting your tax advantages.

3. You need a company that will allow you to maximize cash value growth while minimizing your insurance costs. This is critical!

4. When you take a loan, your money can continue to grow as though you've never borrowed against your policy.

"Basically, here's what happens," Michael explains. "You buy a properly structured cash value life policy that you agree to pay into each month. You are contractually promised a guaranteed amount of growth every year—even if you borrow from it and even when you take an income from it during retirement. You've got a predictable financial vehicle: It's guaranteed for life, and your principal is guaranteed, so you won't lose it during market swings. And you get what we call 'living benefits' from a 7702 Plan™"

There are actually several other Safe Money options you can use, depending on your situation and your goals. There are also Income for Life Safe Money Plans that can guarantee you never outlive your money. This can mean great peace of mind for folks going into retirement. There are also what we call 'super-charged' 7702 Plans™ that allow you to experience the ups of market growth without the risk. This is really exciting, and we'll cover it in a subsequent chapter.

Let's say you buy the finest-quality chocolate bar available (representing term life insurance). You love chocolate and would like nothing more than to sink your teeth into that bar, but the people from whom you bought it say you can't do that. By law, you have to put it away. You can't touch it. It won't go to waste, though. As soon as you die, your heirs get to savor that chocolate bar on the way home from your funeral.

Who wants to buy a chocolate bar they can't even enjoy? You sure wouldn't want to pay much for it, would you? That's why term life is so popular: it costs less. In fact, it's the smallest amount of money you can invest and still provide *some* money for your heirs. But take a look at the reason it costs so much less—it's only in effect for a specified length of time, and it provides benefits only to your heirs. There's no benefit to you.

Okay, back to the chocolate bar metaphor. Now, say you buy the finest-quality chocolate bar available (representing cash value life insurance). This time, though, you're able to savor that chocolate bar while you're still alive. In fact, your chocolate bar keeps getting bigger and bigger—so not only do you get to *keep* enjoying it, but when you die, your heirs will have even more chocolate to enjoy together. And while they're enjoying the smooth sweetness, they'll do so with the satisfaction of knowing you enjoyed it too.

Just go to www.safemoneyretirementbook.com to get a free analysis from a Safe Money Associate of what type of Safe Money plan will be right for you.

From here on, when we—and Michael—talk about cash value insurance, we're talking about the kind of 7702 Plan™ that provides these powerful benefits to you— offered by the kind of companies we work with. Just about anyone can use it (you don't need to be educated or experienced) and it can work on autopilot (you don't have to watch the market, reassess stocks based on performance, or worry about tax consequences). And while it requires a bit of patience, it can work whether you have thousands or just a few hundred to contribute.

Now, let's get back to the story.

"So far it's sounding pretty good," says Susan, "but what do you mean by *living benefits?*"

"I've already mentioned a few," Michael responds. "The 7702 Plan™ gives you growth that is guaranteed by the insurance company to accumulate cash while being immune from whatever the stock market is doing. Another benefit is taxes. The IRA expert Ed Slott says, 'Life insurance is the single biggest benefit to the IRS tax code.' [26] You save taxes on the growth of your principal, you can access the cash value without paying taxes, and when the death benefit is paid out to your heirs, it comes to them income-tax free in most cases because you paid taxes on the money before you put it into your policy.

"And remember that one of the risks of 401(k) plans and mutual funds is the risk that the government could change the rules midstream due to the latest political agenda or bureaucratic whim," Michael says. "With a 7702 Plan™, your policy is a private contract between you and the insurance company.

"Of course, one of the greatest living benefits is your ability to reduce or totally stop paying interest to banks and Finance Your Own Prosperity™," Michael explains.

"How does that work?" Jason asks.

"We'll use a car for example. Let's say you want to buy a $20,000 car. You can get a loan from a bank or car financing company, or in your case, use your 7702 Plan™ to finance the car.

"With traditional car financing, you might finance the car for five years or so. In the end, you have a car paid off and you've lost all the interest and principal to the finance company. When you Finance Your Own Prosperity™, you take the cash out of your 7702 Plan™ and pay for the car in cash. (Often, paying cash can save you money on the purchase price by itself.) Then you make payments back to your policy. This is where it gets exciting—after the five years, you've got your car paid off, but you also have the $20,000 back into your own 7702 Plan™!

"Plus, you can pay additional interest on your payments and the extra money will go to increase your cash value. This is why we call it Finance Your Own Prosperity™, because each time you take out a loan and pay it back with extra interest, it actually increases your cash value."

"That sounds interesting!" Susan says.

"With a cash value insurance policy," Michael continues, "you have access to the cash value in your policy, and you can't be turned down for a loan. If you need to borrow the cash value from your policy, just say the word. No credit check, no tax returns, no qualifying hassle. And no one is going to raise your interest rate if you're late on a payment. In fact, *you* determine the repayment timetable, and *you* decide how often and for how long you want to make payments."

"This almost sounds too good to be true," Jason says.

"It gets even better," Michael responds. "Remember when we talked about how one of the enemies of wealth is interest? When you use your 7702 Plan™ to finance your purchases, your money continues to grow at the same guaranteed rate, as though you never touched a dime. When you pay the loan back, you recoup the cost of that purchase back into your policy, rather than making payments to someone else. You can enjoy some of the things you'd like without destroying your nest egg."

By this time, Jason and Susan are both wide-eyed. "There's got to be a hitch," Susan says, "and I can think of a big one. I'm not sure we'd even qualify for insurance right now. I just had some really serious health problems."

"If you're too old or have health issues that might make you uninsurable, you're not out of luck," Michael explains. "You can buy a policy on a child, spouse, or grandchild who does qualify to be insured. You own the policy, and you still control it so you decide what happens to the money. So let's assume you can qualify. If your policy is structured properly, your policy is permanent. That means as long as you keep it in force, it will be with you forever. This is extremely important when it comes to taxes. Life insurance is one of the best estate-tax planning vehicles there is because it gets paid to your estate income tax free."

Michael adds, "That's another one of the great benefits: your life is insured. The average man in this country has an economic value of more than $1 million dollars. If you die, especially if you die early, your family could suffer a significant economic loss on top of the emotional sorrow of losing you. Insurance provides financially for those you leave behind. In fact, as long as it's in force, your policy will generally pay out a lump-sum income-tax-free death benefit that's far larger than the total contributions you made to your plan.

"Now keep in mind, as we're referencing Finance Your Own Prosperity™, we're talking about policy loans, not withdrawals. Withdrawals are when you permanently take the money out of the policy. We use loans because your money continues to grow even while you are using it. Then, as you pay it back, it is there for you to use again and again.

"The idea is to be able to structure the loans so they can be paid back, similar to a regular car loan. If, for some reason, you can't make payments for a while, it's not a huge deal. No one will be knocking on your door to collect. You simply resume paying when you can. However, you definitely want to pay the loans back if you are using them to Finance Your Own Prosperity™."

"But what happens if we can't, for some reason?" Susan asks.

"You will continue to pay interest on the loan, and ultimately the policy could cancel. Just like gardening—if you stop watering a plant, it stops growing. We want to keep nurturing the 7702 Plan™ so it continues to grow. Then, once you hit your retirement years, we can structure your policy so it is paid up and you never have to pay more into it. It can then be there to provide retirement income.

"But," Michael says, "here's the real beauty of a loan from your plan: *you* structure the repayment schedule. *You* determine how much you can pay and how often you want to pay."

"Makes sense, but is there a limit to how much we can contribute?" Jason asks.

"Yes," Michael says. "We want to make sure that your plan doesn't become a Modified Endowment Contract (MEC). In order to enjoy the maximum tax benefits of your 7702 Plan™, you want to keep the policy within the MEC limit. The IRS has set up guidelines that dictate how much cash value you can put into a policy compared to the insurance amount. If you exceed their limits, meaning you put in too much cash, it could have negative tax implications—essentially ruining one of the major benefits for getting a 7702 Plan™. As Safe Money Associates, we are trained on how to structure the 7702 Plan™ so you stay under the MEC limit to enjoy maximum tax advantages."

"Yeah," Jason replies, "I can see why we want to work with someone who's been trained to do this properly. I'd hate to lose out on tax savings just because of an untrained advisor."

"If this is so great," Susan chimes in, "why haven't I heard anything about it? Is it because it's new?"

"Absolutely not," Michael answers. "In fact, Americans have been using 7702 Plan™-type permanent life insurance policies for over 100 years. Large companies, business people, and average citizens protect their capital by buying cash value life insurance policies on their employees and then using these cash value life insurance policies as safe money foundations. One reason why you might not have heard about it is that gurus, bankers, and Wall Street have no interest in promoting 7702 Plans™ because they often want you to invest in the market."

"Okay." Jason nods. "So how do we get started?"

"The bottom line is this," Michael explains. "You can start funding a 7702 Plan™ using a special type of cash value insurance life policy. Then, instead of borrowing from a bank, you borrow from your policy. You simply use a different way to pay for things—a method that lets you recoup the cost of large purchases, instead of letting that money go into a lender's pocket. And all the while you're growing a tidy nest egg, one you can predict and, even better, one you can count on."

"That *sounds* good," Susan agrees, "but I'm not sure I understand. Why not just put my money in an interest-bearing savings account and then use that money to buy the things I want? Wouldn't I actually come out ahead in the long run?"

"First," Michael replies, "how much does your money grow in a bank account while you aren't using it for something else? 1.5 - 2%, if you are lucky? If you invest in a bond or CD, the percentage of growth will be a little higher. Now consider this: with a 7702 Plan™, not only can your money grow at a guaranteed rate, but if you structure it right—and as a professional, I know how to do it right—you could also receive growth when the market goes up without risking your money in the market.

"But here's the part of the answer that's really convincing," Michael continues. "Let's say you deposit your money in a bank account, and then withdraw the $20,000 we talked about to pay cash for a car. Does the bank continue to pay you interest on the money you withdrew? Of course not. But guess what? Your 7702 Plan™ policy *does*. That's the amazing thing about a 7702

Plan™. People really think it's too good to be true, yet it is true, and it can be a great financial tool for those who take advantage of it."

"I've got to admit, I'm pretty stunned by all this," Jason says. "I just went through a pretty big hassle with the 401 (k) deal—are there rules here? I mean, what kinds of things can I borrow money for?"

"You can borrow from your account for anything you want," Michael answers. "You can run many of your large purchases through it—cars, vacations, business expenses, home improvement, and even real estate purchases. It's your money, and no one is going to tell you what you can do with it."

"So, it's like our own source of financing," Susan says. "But we set the terms and have more control over it."

"Exactly," says Michael. "In the end, what your 7702 Plan™ really can give you is a plan you can count on, a foundation for your financial plan without risking your principal or worrying about what the market is doing, or getting access to your money if something comes up. It's a predictable and safe way to put away your money. Following this plan could ultimately create millions of dollars in wealth for you and your family, while at the same time allowing you to reduce the amount of interest you are paying to banks."

The relief on Jason's face is obvious. "After what we've been through, this would really allow me to sleep well at night," he says.

"Absolutely." Michael responds. "You don't even have to wait until you retire. You get to enjoy the benefits now.

For example, if you want to take a family vacation next year, just get started now. When the time comes, you pull out a couple thousand dollars and go. Then pay the loan back and you recoup the cost of that vacation and it's there for you when you need it next time."

"So we can use it for the kitchen remodel we're thinking of doing too, huh?" says Susan.

"Absolutely," Michael replies. "Home improvement, college, cars, even investing in a business or real estate— whatever you want. Then, when you're ready to retire, you can take withdrawals and loans without having to pay taxes on that money as long as it is structured properly."

"I'm pretty much sold," Jason says, and Susan nods. "But as you can imagine, we don't have a lot of cash on hand right now. How much do we have to invest to get started?"

"The cost to you is only the amount you want to pay in premiums," Michael says. "There are several different ways to get started. Some folks roll over their current 401(k) plans, some move part of their savings over—in fact, there are many different ways to find money to fund a 7702 Plan™. There's no determined amount you have to start with."

"But we have to make monthly premium payments, right?" asks Susan.

"Not necessarily," says Michael. "It's very flexible. You could pay all up front, pay yearly, or even set up what I call an 'automatic Safe Money machine'. This would automatically transfer money from your bank account and pay your premiums each month without you worrying about it. But I imagine the real question you were trying to ask is how you're going to come up with the extra money. That's something specific I want to talk over with you. There are quite a few places I can help you find money to fund your plan. I'm confident that you can easily—and probably painlessly—divert money from other sources to build your plan without changing your lifestyle. Let's start with the most obvious: how much money do you get back on tax returns each year?"

Jason says, "About $4,000 - $5,000."

"Okay, so that's about $400 extra dollars every month you are sending to the IRS for no reason. Is there a reason you like to let Uncle Sam use your money for 12 months without paying you a dime of interest on it?"

"Well, when you put it like that, no, I guess it's not a good idea, is it? I just don't want to have to pay extra when the tax time comes around," Jason finishes.

"I understand. It's easy to set your deductions so that you still get a small refund while allowing most of your money to stay with you to use throughout the year. If you add up the $4,000 - $5,000 for the next 15-20 years of your working life, that could be an extra $100,000 you could put into your plan."

"Well, sheesh," Susan breaks in, "We should do that immediately!"

"We can build a plan that works for you. One client bought cash value policies on each of his boys when they were very young. At the time, his intention was to accumulate some cash, but to also provide them with death benefit coverage when they became adults and responsible for their individual families. As it turns out, one is now married with one daughter. He has cash value that can be used for his daughter's college expenses, braces, family vacations, or new cars. The young son, who is still single, has cash value to continue his college degree, replace his vehicle when the time comes, or make a down payment on a home."

"So we could set these up for our kids as well?" Susan asks.

"Yes. In fact, once they get their own plan in place, many people end up with multiple plans in the family. Kids can use them for college funding options, or to pay for their first car or house," Michael replies.

"So, once we get started, can we start using the money right away, or do we have to wait?" Jason asks.

"Usually you can access your cash value within a couple weeks. You could use it right away to fund that remodeling project you've been talking about.

"It's important to realize that a 7702 Plan™ is not a get-rich-quick scheme," emphasizes Michael. "It's a long-term plan to put you on the path to being able to retire with Safe Money. It requires diligence and patience."

"If by using your plan, we were able to cut back on some of the areas we're currently wasting, changing my withholdings so I keep more of my tax money throughout the year, and redirecting my $550 per month 401(k) contributions, that's about $400 per month on taxes, $550 on our current 401(k), and we're wasting another $50 per month right now on an extra landline phone we don't use. So how much could we have if we contributed about $1000 per month into a policy?" Jason asks.

How to Find Money to Fund a 7702 Plan™

1. I'll have that back, thank you. How much is your tax refund each year? Think about changing your deductions to keep more of your income instead of letting the IRS use it for a full year before giving it back to you.

2. Redirect your cash flow. Often you can redirect money currently going into poorly performing or risky market investments into a 7702 Plan™.

3. Make your money go to work for you. Often funding a plan with extra money you've got in the bank makes sense because you are getting guaranteed growth and still have access to it.

4. Get off the roller coaster. This may be a no-brainer if you have money in stocks or mutual funds. Consider moving some money out of the market if you are tired of the roller coaster.

5. Withdraw from 401(k) and IRA. IRAs and 401(k)s could become a tax-time bomb when you start taking money out. They often have exposure to the stock market downturns as well. Your 7702 Plan™ may allow you to eliminate unknown taxation when you start taking distributions and can secure your money from risk in the market. (Please consult with your tax professional and a qualified advisor before withdrawing from qualified plans.)

6. Stop the expenses. When they add it all up, people are often shocked at how much extra they are paying in insurance, utilities, and other everyday expenses. Making some minor lifestyle changes, or just doing a little research on reducing current expenses, can help you build up your 7702 Plan™ and get on the path of Safe Money.

7. In force insurance policies. Many people have existing life insurance policies that are not structured as effectively as possible. You may be able to do a

> 1035 exchange that keeps the cash value and the tax benefits you currently have while improving your results.
>
> **8. Chopping away at debt.** Instead of slowly chopping away at debt, consider funding a 7702 Plan™ and then taking a chunk of money and paying off the balance of a credit card. This could save you a substantially amount on interest costs.
>
> **9. Splurge on your future.** Instead of taking the money from your tax return and buying that big screen TV or trip, consider funding a 7702 Plan™ and building on your financial future.
>
> **10. Extra mortgage payments.** If you are currently making extra payments to your mortgage principal, consider putting that into a plan where growth is guaranteed while also giving you access to that cash without having to qualify for a loan in order to use it.

"Good question. This is the true beauty of the Safe Money 7702 Plan™—it allows us to put money away and know with relative certainty how much is going to be there for you when you need it."

Susan chimes in. "Yeah, I'm really tired of opening our 401(k) statement and seeing it go down, down, down!"

"Usually, a 7702 Plan™ performs best the longer you let it grow and compound. When do you think you will want to start taking money out?" Michael asks.

"Well, let's say age 65," Jason replies.

After crunching a few numbers, Michael says, "Assuming that you get average growth of 7-8% using the indexing strategy (we'll cover this in a second) at the age of 65, you could have right around $800,000, with a death benefit of approximately $1.1 million that could go to your spouse or children. But here's the real exciting part . . . are you ready?" [27]

"Yeah. What have you got?"

"Using these projections, at age 65, you could have an annual cash flow, that you can access without a taxable event, of $97,000 until age 100."

"$97,000 per year . . . that I get without a taxable event? Wow, that's amazing, especially considering it's not going to get wiped out in a market downturn, and we know we can count on it being safe," Susan says.

"$97,000 per year for 35 years is like 3 million dollars! How is that possible?" Jason says.

"Remember that when you borrow against your policy, the cash value continues to grow as if it's never been touched. It's also important to remember these projections are done using the insurance companies' actuarial projections. They use data from the past 25 years . . . but they aren't guaranteed. There's a chance it could be less than that."

Susan jumps in. "I appreciate you saying that. I hate to be sold a bill of goods only to be disappointed. Even if it's half that amount, having about $45,000 per year to live on until age 100 is pretty fantastic. Plus, that money isn't at risk in the market. But $1000 might be pushing it for us right now. What would happen if we only did, say, $500 per month?"

"No problem," Michael says. "With $500 per month, you're still potentially looking at $48,000 every year until age 100. You don't pay tax on this money because you are borrowing against the policy, not withdrawing the money out of the policy. Of course, this is the way it works under the current IRS tax laws.

"Keep in mind," continues Michael, "these policies work with compound interest. That means that the more money you put into your policy, the faster your policy grows. Why wouldn't you want to put as much money as much as possible into a policy that only gets better the more you put in? With traditional investments like 401(k)s or mutual funds, there is no direct correlation between the amount you contribute and improving results. A 7702 Plan™ gets better as you contribute more and more. In fact, it grows exponentially, meaning the growth maximizes when you need it most during your later years."

"Interesting. So we should consider finding ways to increase the amount we pay in because we'll get better results that way?" Susan asks.

"Exactly," Michael adds. "Plus, don't forget that you can access that money without having to pay taxes on it under the current IRS tax codes—as long as you structure the policy correctly. That's why working with a trained Safe Money Associate is so important. If you don't do it right, you could have lose major tax benefits or miss out on maximizing your cash value growth. This is too important to trust to someone who hasn't had the proper training."

As we step away from the table, it is clear that Jason and Susan are off to a good start on their journey to retiring with Safe Money. But as we leave them to the beginning of their new financial life, we have some shocking revelations to show you.

In the next chapter, we'll show you what might just be the most exciting part of this whole process.

Jason and Susan can potentially have such a great cash flow in retirement because they are using the Indexing strategy with a 7702 Plan™. This allows them to participate when the market goes up . . . but never risk their money to loss when it comes down. That's exactly what you'll see in the next chapter.

CHAPTER 8

SUPER CHARGING
THE 7702 PLAN™

"The first rule of investing is NEVER LOSE MONEY.
The second rule is NEVER forget rule #1."
— Warren Buffett

I've always wanted to fly. Not in a plane, hot air balloon, or with the help of something man-made. I simply want to look up and take off flying through the air. Unfortunately, I haven't figured out how to make that happen—like the old saying goes: "What goes up must come down." I learned that the hard way jumping off the bunk bed as a kid.

As we've discussed, this up-and-down phenomenon is not limited to physics—it happens quite frequently on the stock market as well. We can have some exhilarating rides up only to suffer financial broken bones when the market comes crashing back down. But it doesn't have to be that way. In this chapter, I'm going to show you how you may just be able to defy market gravity.

One of the most exciting things about a 7702 Plan™ is that you can supercharge the cash value portion of your insurance policy by using a special indexing strategy. The indexing strategy can allow you to enjoy the upside growth of the market without ever risking your money to market losses! (You can go up without coming down!)

In other words, the 7702 Plan™ indexing strategy could give you double-digit returns on up years when the market gains, without the downside risk!

This means when the market goes up, your money can grow (I'll explain more in just a second) *but when the market goes down, you are protected and your money cannot be lost.* This can be extremely beneficial during times of market turbulence. In years when the market goes up, so do your cash values, and when the market falls, you are protected against that loss. Your money is locked in so you don't lose!

Now, why is this so important?

Because inflation is one of the biggest threats to growing your money and wealth. If inflation is running at 3-5% (or even higher, depending on the government's monetary policy) it's important to have your money outpace inflation.

If your money is growing slower than the rate of inflation, you aren't growing your money—you are actually decreasing the value of it over time! The indexing strategy can allow you to outpace inflation by capitalizing on potential double-digit growth in the years when the market goes up.

Wait a minute.

Didn't I just spend several of the first chapters in this book explaining why the stock market may not be the greatest place to invest your money? Am I changing my tune?

Not at all.

The cash value growth in your 7702 Plan™ indexing policy is *linked* to the S&P 500 or some other index of your choice, but your cash is *not* actually invested *in* the market. That way, your money is always safe and guaranteed by the insurance company.

Remember in Chapter 2 when we showed you the different plunges the market had taken over the years and how long it took to recover and return to even? Now you don't have to deal with that at all!

Your money is protected from any market loss because it is not directly in the market, but at the same time, you participate in the growth of the S&P 500 up to a limit or cap. Let's say the upside cap is 12% (this can vary from plan to plan). This means even if the market goes up 14% or more, your cash value growth would be limited to just 12%.

Having a cap is actually a good thing because this is what allows the insurance company to protect you against losses in those years when the market goes down.

Let's look at a picture that will illustrate this point. This is a hypothetical example of a typical stock market strategy vs. a 7702 Plan™ indexing strategy.

So, let's say you start out with $10,000. And in the first year, the S&P 500 grows by 10%. The first year, there is no difference, and you have $11,000 in either account. In year two, your money grows another 10%. Now you have $12,100 in either account.

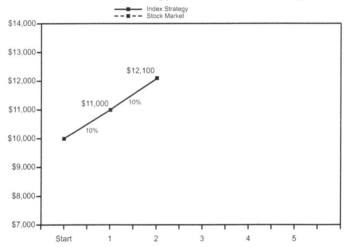

Index Strategy vs. Market Strategy

But let's say that in year three, the S&P 500 drops 20%. Can that happen? Sure it can. The last few years of the 2000s were worse times than that! Now you would have about $9,600 if had you invested directly in the S&P 500. However, in the indexed strategy, your principal and interest are protected against market loss. So, now instead of $9,600, you hold at $12,100.

In year four, the market drops another 17%. Now, instead of having $9,600, you have around $7,900. In the indexed strategy, you're still on hold at $12,100.

Now here's the million-dollar question: Do you want $7,900 or $12,100?

That's quite a difference, and it's clear from this example that losing principal can be financially devastating. That's

Index Strategy vs. Market Strategy

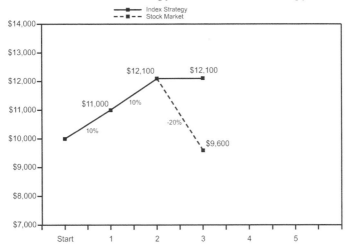

why Warren Buffet said, "It's not so much about the return *on* your money as the return *of* your money." When you lose principal, you've got to get big-time results to bring it back to even.

Index Strategy vs. Market Strategy

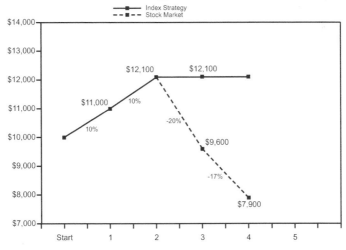

Now let's look at what happens when the market rebounds. Let's say in year five, the market grows by 15%. In the stock market strategy, the $7,900 would get the full 15% growth, which is about $1,100, so your cash value would climb back up to a little over $9,000. In the indexed strategy, your money would only grow by 12% (remember we have a cap) to $13,550. But even with the capped growth, you have $13,550 versus $9,000!

Again, quite a difference.

Index Strategy vs. Market Strategy

In this example, the downsides of the stock market strategy were:

- After five years, you end up with less money than you started with.

- From the end of year 4 to year 5, it would take a 30% return to get you back to your original $10,000 (and how likely is that to happen in *one* year?)

- Even if you did get the 30% you needed, it will only bring you back to $10,000. You just lost *five* years and you are just barely back to even.

Can you see why the 7702 Plan™ indexing strategy is so exciting? Now you can have your money growing when the market goes up, you could outpace inflation with potential double-digit gains, and you never have to worry about losing money when the market goes down.

What kind of peace of mind would that give you, knowing that your money is always safe?

Now what would happen if the market goes down for 10 years in a row?

Many of the 7702 Plan™ policies can be set up so that there is a guaranteed amount of growth credited to your policy cash values, which guarantees that even if you don't achieve growth in the market, your cash value can continue to grow. (Every plan is a little bit different. That's why it's so important to work with a trained Safe Money Associate who can show you your options.)

The rest of the 7702 Plan™ benefits still work the same. Meaning, you can Finance Your Own Prosperity™ by accessing your cash value for cars, college, or other major purchases. *Some financial products can even guarantee an income you will never outlive.* Be sure to ask your Safe Money Associate about this!

Now, with all this being said, indexed life insurance doesn't have to be where you put all your money, but for many people, it is an excellent way to position a portion of your portfolio to enjoy the ups of the market without the downside risk.

This is obviously a brief introduction to the indexing strategy. To learn more about how this works, just request a 7702 Plan™ Blueprint at the end of this book and a Safe Money Associate can help you see it in action and answer your questions.

The Wrap

The indexed strategy makes sense for people who want to avoid market risk, but still want the possibility of double-digit gains and all the other benefits that a 7702 Plan™ can give them.

Using this strategy, you could save more money even without changing your current lifestyle by repositioning some of your assets from being deposited into accounts that are taxed during retirement to an indexed life insurance policy.

The supercharged 7702 Plan™ indexing strategy could allow you to:

- Participate in double-digit gains in up years

- Help outpace inflation

- Grow your money tax deferred

- Access cash values without incurring tax

- Provide cash flow for life

In the next chapter, we'll show you exactly how cash value life insurance impacted the lives of men and women just like you. You'll also recognize some of the biggest names in business that used their cash value life insurance to build their wealth.

Turn the page to see if you recognize a few of these people who, like many of our Safe Money retirees, used the living benefits of life insurance to growth their wealth.

SECTION 4

SAFE: EXAMPLES IN ACTION

*"People seldom improve when they have no other model but
themselves to copy after."*

— Oliver Goldsmith

CHAPTER 9

DISNEY, J.C. PENNEY, MCDONALD'S, AND YOU: MAKING IT WORK

"Though no one can go back and make a brand-new start, anyone can start from now and make a brand-new ending."
— Carl Bard

Holly is a 42-year-old New Yorker and a single mother of two. She has a steady job working in an HR department, earning about $33,000 per year, and is having a hard time making ends meet.

Her two kids are in the "expensive" stage of life—middle school and high school—where it seems like every time you turn around, there's another expense.

She's running ragged taking care of two kids, working full-time, paying the bills, and keeping the house in order.

It's almost too much for any one person to handle.

Add to it the fact that she's in a seemingly insurmountable amount of debt, and Holly doesn't feel like she's ever going to get out of the hole she's in.

She sees no light at the end of the tunnel—no way out!

But it gets worse.

She was actually in more debt than she realized. After totaling up all the credit cards, lines of credit with stores, and the student loans, her debt total, not including her car or home, was over $59,000. She knew it was bad, but this was a real eye-opener. That was two years' worth of her salary, and $59,000 did not even count her car or home debt.

She was contributing $100 per month to a company retirement plan, but she knew that was not going to give her the financial independence she wanted.

The rest of her paycheck each month was going to pay bills or pay down credit card and student loan debt.

When we asked her what three financial goals she had, her reply was a lot like you might guess. First, she'd like to have a little money set aside to take a break and breathe for a weekend or so.

Next, she wanted to get out of debt and have some emergency savings put away just in case something came up with her or her kids.

And lastly, she wanted to be able to save money for her kids' college funds and her own retirement.

With only $33,000 in income, $59,000 in consumer debt, and college loans, two kids, and a mortgage, doesn't this seem like a hopeless case?

Left to her own devices, she really was hopeless. She didn't know what to do, and she didn't feel there was any way out of her current situation.

That's where we came in. After reviewing her debts, expenses, and current retirement contributions, we helped Holly put together a 7702 Plan™, which included a spending and debt analysis. Through that process, we helped Holly find and put away over $500 per month she didn't know she had.

Over $500 per month on just a $33,000 per year salary!

Plus, she was able to redirect her current retirement contributions that were currently at risk in the market into an indexed 7702 Plan™ insurance policy to create a nest egg she can count on. She has literally started down the Safe Money path to retirement.

This might seem hard to believe, but the exciting part is that based on the insurance company projections, by the time she turns 65, she could potentially take out $68,000 per year, every year until age 100! Plus, as long as she does it properly, that money can be accessed without incurring tax!

Imagine her relief when we gave her the 7702 Plan™ Blueprint that showed her how, using just her current income, she could create a simple plan to follow.

This process helped her get out of debt, get her spending under control, and ultimately, gave her hope because she now has a plan for financial independence.

By steadily putting away money each month, she could have the security of knowing that after age 65, she could have as much as $68,000 per year on just a $33,000 income! Plus, when she does pass on, she'll have a death benefit payable to her two children because of her life insurance policy!

JC Penney

In 1898, James Cash Penney was working in a Golden Rule Store, which was one shop in a small chain of dry goods stores. He turned out to be such an enterprising worker that the pair of owners took him under their wing, offering him a one-third partnership in a new store they were opening. James managed to scrape together $2,000—a pretty significant sum in those days—and opened the new store in Kemmerer, Wyoming.

During the next five years, James helped open two more stores and was doing very well. James focused his efforts on the stores, even investing the extra money he made by working as a lumberjack. By 1912, he was running 34 stores throughout the Rocky Mountain region.

The next year, James moved his company headquarters to Salt Lake City, Utah, and incorporated under a name you'll easily recognize: The J.C. Penney Company. The chain exploded and by 1929, there were 1,400 stores throughout the nation.

Then things got interesting. The stock market crashed, and the nation was plunged into the depths of the Great Depression. The Depression devastated his stores and his wealth. He was in financial ruin.

Luckily, James had not risked all of his money in the market. He had built a Safe Money foundation. To rebound from the difficult times, he took out a loan from his cash value life insurance policies. He used the cash to meet day-to-day and payroll expenses for his chain of stores. Not only did he keep his head above water, but he also rebounded. Today, the stores take in revenues nationwide of $18.5 billion a year.

As it turns out, that simple cash loan had a greater impact than even James could have realized. Ever heard of Walmart? On a 1940 visit to a J.C. Penney store in Des Moines, Iowa, James patiently trained a young employee, Sam Walton, showing him how to gift-wrap packages using the least amount of ribbon needed to do the job—and another retail giant was born.

Dr. Jeff

Jeff thought he was doing pretty well.

He was fifty years old, making a great income as a doctor, and putting $1,000 into his 401(k) every month. On top of that, Jeff had over $110,000 already socked away. Of course, he wasn't really thrilled that he'd recently lost a big chunk of it in the market crash of 2008, yet despite this setback, he thought he was still on track for a great lifestyle.

He wanted financial independence at age 60, and he figured if he could have $70,000-$80,000 per year to live for the rest of his life, he could hang it up whenever he wanted to after 60. He was also afraid inflation was going to continue to eat away at his savings. Jeff wanted to make sure that he could provide his own retirement cash flow. He didn't want to count on social security because, according to the Congressional Budget Office, in 2011 the Social Security Administration was already running a 45-billion-dollar deficit. And at the end of the day, he wanted to be in control of his finances and retirement, not leave it to someone else.

SAFE MONEY - BRENT TYCKSEN

You could say Jeff thought he had it all under control. In his mind, he was doing everything right. Until he saw the truth.

You see, most people have no idea how long their money will actually last after they stop working.

Jeff crunched some quick numbers. He already had $110,000 saved. Plus, he was adding $1,000 per month to his 401(k). The result was shocking. He discovered that if he continued on his current path, he would only have about $30,000 per year during retirement. And this was BEFORE taxes! Assuming he's in a 28% tax bracket, that's more like $23,400 per year or $2,000 per month!

Right now Jeff is living off $10,000 per month, so living off just $2,000 per month was like a cold bucket of water right in the face.

But that's not all.

There are other problems with Jeff's current plan.

The money in his current retirement plan is fully taxable. Like we already showed above, the $30,000 gets taxed when he pulls it out to use it. Plus, if he dies before he retires, his income stops and he won't have the money built up to provide for his wife or family— there are no guarantees or death benefit. The money is at risk in the market, and the money is tied up in a qualified government plan.

But it gets worse.

This is what really shocked him: For his 80th birthday present, he would be looking at an empty retirement account! That's right—his $2,000 per month would be gone by the time he was 80.

Remember, Jeff wants to retire at age 60.

Using the Lifestyle Income Estimator on our www.safemoneyretirementbook.com, we showed him that his $2,000 per month could actually run out in less than 20 years!

According to *US News and World Report*, once a man reaches 65 years old, his life expectancy is 83 years, and one in every four will live past age 90. [28]

He wondered what type of lifestyle he was going to have with just $2,000 per month, living with the fear that the money would run out all too soon.

So, we looked at some other options for him.

By using a 7702 Plan™ and working with an Safe Money Associate—a specialist in helping people secure cash flow that they won't outlive—we came up with a solution that excited and delighted him.

Jeff wanted to see what his retirement would look like if he redirected the $1,000 from his 401(k) into an indexed cash value insurance policy.

We also showed him how to use a rule in the tax code to roll some of his money out of his 401(k) without penalties. He could then use this money to fund his indexed cash value insurance policy, which would safeguard his money against market downturns. (This needs to be suitable for the client.)

He was comfortable using one of our 7702 Plan™ Insurance Companies because this particular one has been around for over 300 years and has nearly 600 billion dollars in assets around the globe.

After implementing the 7702 Plan™ indexing strategies, Jeff was amazed and excited at his new financial independence plan.

Remember, in his current situation, he was looking at running out of money after 15 to 20 years. Plus, this income was fully taxable, didn't have any guarantees, and it was at risk in the market.

With the Indexed 7702 Plan™, his new plan could give him approximately $69,000 per year—for the rest of his life! And as long as he follows the IRS code properly, he could access that cash flow without a taxable event (according to current IRS tax code).

But that's not all.

In his new 7702 Plan™, he has no market risk, and if he dies too soon, his family will be protected with the life insurance death benefit. Plus, he has access to the cash value in his insurance policy to finance himself to wealth throughout his life!

Like we mentioned before, Jeff was excited about $70,000 per year compared to $24,000, and delighted when he saw this new plan. Wouldn't you be?

What if you are already in your late fifties or even sixties and don't have a plan like Jeff has? Is it too late?

Thankfully, it's not. There are still many options for people of any age, but it's important to start now, and not let another day go by without implementing the Safe Money plan. Get started today at:

www.safemoneyretirementbook.com.

Walt Disney

The second household name you'll no doubt recognize involves a man who fought all odds to follow his dream: Walt Disney. [29] Walt and his brother, Roy, were in the animation business. Their story is almost hard to believe. One of their most popular characters was stolen by another studio. Their best animator jumped ship. Their studio was chronically understaffed and almost always in debt. In fact, Walt Disney struggled financially for years on the brink of bankruptcy—actually going bankrupt at the age of 21.

Fast-forward to the early 1950s. The only amusement parks in the entire country were horrifically dilapidated places peppered with rusting, creaky rides and known only for their filthy restrooms and the drunks who always hung around. Walt dreamed instead of an immaculately clean amusement park filled with imaginative rides—a place where families weren't afraid to eat the food. World War II had just ended, and the nation was licking its wounds. Walt dreamed of creating an amusement park with an idealistic Main Street, U.S.A., where families could identify with something wholesome and good. But that's not all: he dreamed of charging admission to his park and actually making a profit.

Everyone to whom he presented his idea thought he was crazy—and told him so. After all, *no one* charged admission to an amusement park. That just wasn't done. And amusement parks simply couldn't be family-friendly—everyone knew you'd have to sell alcohol if you wanted a prayer of staying afloat. Even his brother Roy—also his business partner and financial manager—told him it couldn't be done. He urged Walt to forget it. After all, they were in the animation business, not the amusement park business.

Determined to achieve his dream, Walt had no choice but to move ahead on his own. Turned down by traditional financing, he emptied his savings account, sold his vacation home in Palm Springs, and recruited the help of a few employees who shared his vision. Then, he used a loan from his cash value insurance policies to help finance the park. (Roy later admitted he had no idea where Walt's money was coming from, but decided not to ask.)

What happened to Walt's dream? Disneyland opened on September 8, 1955, with 18 attractions. It welcomed half a million visitors in the first month it was open. By the end of its first year, it had hosted more than 3.5 million guests. Less than three years later, it welcomed its ten millionth visitor—a number that exceeded well-known national landmarks like Yellowstone and the Grand Canyon. Today, its California park alone—with more than 60 attractions—has been visited by more than 600 million guests from throughout the world. A dozen of the original attractions from 1955 are still operating in the park today as a testament to Walt Disney's dream of a high-quality, enduring adventure for families.

Robert G.

Robert distinctly remembers the day he first knew that nothing could stop him. He had landed a great-paying sales job, and he was also less than a year away from graduating with a degree in business. He was finally on his way up.

It had been a busy year for Robert. In fewer than 12 months, he had sold his old home—for a tidy profit—and finished building his family's new home. Just as they were unpacking the boxes, his wife announced that they were expecting a baby. They were delighted! Robert knew life would change, and that his cost of living would go up with another mouth to feed, but the idea of his growing family only motivated him to work all the harder.

Life seemed to be moving in the right direction for Robert.

He'd been with the company for almost a year when the recession of 2008 caused the economy to plummet. The medical specialty that Robert served was hit particularly hard. Things started to get tough. His income was going down, but his costs weren't.

With his wife at home, caring for their new baby, and with only one income to support the family, money became tight for the first time in their marriage.

Robert went from comfort and a sense of security to just the opposite. In just 12 months, he went from having $15,000 in the bank to having $15,000 in credit card debt. He went from the joy of building a new home to the fear of losing that home. He went from a feeling of being unstoppable to a gripping sensation of worry. He despaired of ever being able to climb out of debt and replace his savings.

Robert now had an empty bank account, a whopping credit card debt, two ailing cars, and a home on the verge of being foreclosed. He faced the embarrassment of losing his house, disappointing his family, and starting over. The last straw was his final few weeks at his job—his last three paychecks bounced because the company didn't have the funds to pay him.

Sound hopeless?

It could have been. But something changed for Robert—and it's the same kind of thing that can change for you. He went back to the drawing board.

Robert's biggest paradigm shift was realizing the difference between saving and investing: *saving* is putting your money where you don't risk losing it. *Investing* is putting your money where you might lose it all.

Robert also wanted to grow his money while protecting it from taxes. He finally found the solution he was looking for: a 7702 Plan™. He took what little money he received from his tax refund and started a 7702 Plan™. Despite the terrible economic situation, it changed his entire outlook.

In his own words: "I could create a crystal-clear picture of what my financial future would look like. I could have money in case of emergency or capital in case a good investment opportunity came up. I could use my 7702 Plan™ to pay for vacations, get out of debt, and send my kids to college or pay for my retirement.

"A 7702 Plan™ gave me a sense of security and gratification, knowing that my money would grow and be available for my use and that my family would be protected and taken care of in case something should happen to me. I have an idea of what my future will look like, I know how much money I will have at certain milestones in my life, and I have a strong financial foundation on which to continue building."

Doris Christopher

Doris Christopher may not be a name you recognize, but the company she founded will be very familiar. Doris was a successful home economist and educator, but she had a dream. All those hours working with homemakers had convinced her that women needed quality timesaving tools designed to make cooking quick and easy. Women didn't want to spend hours and hours in the kitchen grinding out meals—they wanted to create great meals, quickly, due to their increasingly busy schedules.

Doris not only had a dream—she had a plan.

Doris's plan involved an army of consultants who would do in-home cooking demonstrations using her professional-quality tools and equipment. Tupperware had done it, and with outstanding success—a homemaker schedules a party, invites her friends, and the rest falls into place.

With the support of her husband, Jay, and that of her two young daughters, Doris came up with a detailed business plan and got ready to put it into action. The only thing standing between her and her dream was money.

Her solution was simple. In 1980, Doris borrowed $3,000 from her life insurance policy, and The Pampered Chef® was born in the basement of her suburban Chicago home.

In the ensuing decades, the business moved to a series of progressively larger facilities. By 2002, the company had blossomed into a $700 million enterprise that was acquired by Warren Buffett's Berkshire Hathaway Corporation. Today, The Pampered Chef® has grown into a multimillion-dollar international corporation serving 12 million customers annually—and it all started with the loan from her life insurance policy. [30]

Angie

To protect her privacy, we won't tell you Angie's last name— but her life insurance advisor, Rocky, is happy to tell a convincing story about another aspect of the 7702 Plan™: the legacy we leave to our family when we pass on.

Angie was married to Michael—a 41-year-old anesthesiologist. They were referred to Rocky by another physician, and Rocky met Angie and Michael at their home to discuss their needs. They had a young family— three children under the age of seven. Together they determined they needed $2 million in life insurance coverage.

After a second meeting, during which Michael filled out all the applications, Rocky also signed him up for $10,000 a month in disability insurance.

Everything went well for the next 18 months. Suddenly, Michael started getting sick. His weight plummeted. He became so weak that it was a struggle to work. A battery of tests revealed no cause for his medical problems, and he became desperate. Almost out of options, he finally talked to a colleague who suggested a latex allergy as the possible culprit. Michael was tested, and sure enough, he was allergic to latex. His allergic reaction was behind the host of symptoms that had plagued him.

With a confirmed latex allergy, Michael had to stop working in the hospital. His disability insurance kicked in, providing an income of $10,000 a month. Yearning to still practice medicine, Michael used some of his disability income and part of his cash value life policy to start a pain clinic—a clinic with a strict ban on latex of any kind.

Things went very well for two years. One night, Angie went out to dinner with friends. Michael, who wasn't feeling well, stayed home. That night, Angie found him dead on the bathroom floor. The autopsy results revealed that Michael had contracted bacterial meningitis—and because of the impact that his latex allergy had on his immune system, he didn't have the ability to fight the infection. It killed powerfully and suddenly.

Shortly thereafter, Rocky delivered a $2 million check to Angie—the amount of the death benefit on the cash value life policy she and Michael had purchased just a few years earlier. Nothing can bring Michael back, but Rocky felt a great sense of satisfaction in helping provide a secure financial future for Angie and her children as a result of their life insurance policy.

Ray Kroc

Ray Kroc came from humble beginnings. Born in Chicago in 1902, at the age of 15, he lied about his age and landed himself a job as an ambulance driver for the Red Cross. Later, he actually trained to become an ambulance driver during World War I (where he struck up a friendship with Walt Disney, who was in the same training). Peace treaties were signed before he saw any combat action, so he returned home and tried his hand at a number of jobs—paper-cup salesman, pianist, jazz musician, band member, and radio disk jockey. In a move that would later prove fortuitous, Ray worked at a restaurant in exchange for room and board so he could learn the restaurant business.

In 1954, at the age of 52, as a milkshake machine salesman, Ray took notice of a hamburger stand in San

Bernardino, California. While most restaurants bought one or two Prince Castle Multi-mixers which could each mix five shakes at once, the San Bernardino restaurant had bought eight. Curiosity got the better of Ray Kroc, and he wanted to see what kind of restaurant needed to churn forty milkshakes at a time. And so he set out for California.

What Kroc saw when he got to that restaurant—a hamburger stand owned by Maurice and Richard McDonald—would not only change his life forever, but would change the scene of the fast-food industry throughout the world.

Kroc saw the two legendary golden arches and saw lines of people queued up for the restaurant's simple fare of burgers, fries, and milkshakes.

Ray Kroc wanted to slow down as a traveling salesman. His health was declining. He was suffering from diabetes and arthritis, and he had bigger fish to fry. Ray managed to convince the brothers to sell the McDonald's name and trade secrets to him, and worked a deal to pay for it with a percentage of the receipts.

McDonald's was on its way to becoming a household name. In 1955, Ray opened his first McDonald's drive-in restaurant in Des Plaines, Illinois.

While things inside the restaurants ran smoothly, Ray faced massive challenges with cash flow, franchises, competition, and the economy in general. He was determined to be successful and spent year after year, working day and night, to build his company.

In order to build the largest fast-food chain in the world and overcome constant cash-flow problems, Ray took out loans on two cash value life insurance policies to get his infant company off the ground. He used some of the money to create an enduring advertising campaign that centered on the company's mascot, Ronald McDonald.

Ray Kroc passed away from old age in January, 1984, at the age of 81, just 10 months before McDonald's sold its fifty-billionth hamburger. At the time of his death, there were some 7,500 McDonald's restaurants worldwide. Today, with more than 25,000 restaurants worldwide, McDonald's is the world's largest food-service retailer, with operations in more than 65 countries.

The Wrap

What did you learn from James Cash Penney, Dr. Jeff, Walt Disney, Stephen G., Doris Christopher, Angie, and Ray Kroc? There are important lessons in every one of these examples. You can work as hard as humanly possible. You can make all the right plans. But when the financial storms come, if you have a weak financial foundation, it can be devastating. But if you have the right Safe Money foundation in place, you can withstand them. You can keep your money safely growing outside of the market. You can have the peace of mind you are looking for.

And here's the really great news. It's not hard or complicated. You don't have to know it all.

To see a personalized blueprint of how a 7702 Plan™ could work for you and your unique situation, just use the form in the back of this book or go to www.safemoneyretirementbook.com and fill out a 7702 Plan Blueprint Analysis request, and a Safe Money Associate will work with you to design a custom 7702 Plan for you and your family—*at no cost.* This blueprint can show you how to get on the Safe Money path by helping you get out of debt, save on taxes and eliminate the risk of losing your money in the stock market. By creating a safe money foundation, you can Finance Your Own Prosperity™ and control your financial future.

Remember what you learned from Aristotle in the opening pages of this book: "Money is a guarantee that we may have what we want in the future."

You may not be able to go back in time and change your beginning, but you can start today and make a brand-new ending.

CHAPTER 10

BONUS CHAPTER: FOR BUSINESS OWNERS ONLY

"The entrepreneur is our visionary, the creator in each of us.
We're born with that quality and it defines our lives as we
respond to what we see, hear, feel, and experience."
— Michael Gerber

If there's a portion of the country that is underserved and underappreciated, it might just be the small-business owner.

I know firsthand because I have been one for the better part of a decade and my family has a long genealogy of small-business owners.

It goes all the way back to my great-great-grandfather, who was a tavern owner in Germany.

From there, we have my great-grandfather, who owned several farm and ranch-related businesses, and my grandfather, who owned several construction businesses. Being a business owner is tough.

I know what it's like to have the stress of overhead, payroll, advertising to get new clients, economic forces outside of our control, the late hours, missed soccer games or music recitals, and the huge amount of risk we take on. We do it all because we want to provide financial security for our families and live the American Dream of financial success.

Most of us don't get benefit packages that someone else is paying for. Usually no one is contributing to *our* retirement plan. We don't punch a time clock or have the luxury of having someone else cut us a check every two weeks. It's common knowledge that the small-business owner is the engine of the American economy. Yet too often, we work ourselves to death and continually pour any extra money back into the business, often neglecting our own savings as we try to build our companies.

If you are anything like me, we approach our business with a case of never-ending faith that next week, month, or year, we'll make the money we want. And soon, months and years have passed, and we've invested everything back in the business and haven't stashed anything away for ourselves.

Joining the ranks of the Safe Money plan owners could change that right now.

Not only can a 7702 Plan™ create an "automatic safe money machine" where you put money away each month without thinking about it, but you can still access that money for use *in* your business.

Let's talk about three simple ways you can be using a 7702 Plan™ to save money, prepare for the future, and help your business grow.

Finance Your Own Prosperity™

If you buy equipment, vehicles, own real estate for your business or investments, or provide a service, this is for you.

Funding a 7702 Plan™ can be done a couple different ways.

You can start by simply putting in a set amount of money each month, then borrowing against that cash value to buy whatever you need for your business.

You can also start a plan by dumping in a one-time payment like $20,000, $50,000 or even $100,000 and using that as your own source of funding. It's kind of like your own private source of financing, except no qualifying is necessary to use the cash!

Use your 7702 Plan™ to buy business equipment, vehicles, or real estate by using the money in your plan while it still grows as if you've never touched it. Instead of going out and buying a truck for your company the old way, use your 7702 Plan™ to finance your purchase, then recoup the cost of the truck by paying your insurance loan back.

You can even get more advanced by using these plans as a separate entity that acts as a leasing company that purchases vehicles, real estate, and other equipment.

If the Worst Should Happen

Ever heard of a business getting destroyed because a partner dies and the spouse comes in to take over the interest with no experience whatsoever?

I really do like my business partner's wife, but she and I running a business together would not be a pretty picture.

It happens more often than you might think.

In fact, take a look at these sobering statistics.

These figures show the likelihood, out of 100, that one of two business partners in good health will die prior to 65:

Age of Business Owners	Chances
40/40	35%
45/45	33%
50/50	29.9%
55/55	24.7%

If there are three partners, the percentages are much higher. [31]

So what does that mean for you and your business? If you have a partner, or two, you can use a 7702 Plan™ insurance policy to fund a buy-sell agreement. This would provide you with cash to buy out that partner's ownership of the business if they should die. The company can continue to thrive without the disruption of a new partner and the spouse of the partner will be compensated fairly.

But it gets even better than that.

Let's go for the best-case scenario. Assume you and your partner both live long, healthy lives.

You get to enjoy all the living benefits of the 7702 Plan™ throughout your lives the same way we already have described previously. Use it for vehicle financing, major purchases, funding growth, or buying real estate.

Ride Off Into the Sunset

This is ultimately where you probably want to be.

We've hopefully already established in black and white why a solid foundation of safe money is the key to a great lifestyle— but why not use this powerful tool to grow your business, save you money on interest throughout your life, and then enjoy a passive stream of cash flow that comes from your 7702 Plan™ as you travel to exotic destinations with your spouse, golfing the days away and enjoying the fruits that you worked so hard for?

If all the living benefits weren't enough to convince you that a 7702 Plan™ should be a part of your financial plan, this might.

Willie Sutton and the Tax Man always follow the money.

> "The single biggest benefit in the tax code is the tax exemption for life insurance."
> Ed Slot
> The Retirement Savings Time bomb

Depending on current laws, estate taxes can take a chunk out of your estate, which could include residential and commercial real estate, investments, and all the assets you may have. Often people underestimate their estates, and yet they can add up to $800,000 to $1,000,000 fairly quickly.

Imagine the problem your family could have when they get a tax bill saying they owe $500,000 and much of that is tied up in real estate.

This is especially problematic if the real estate market is down, and people have to "fire sell" at below market value just to satisfy the demands of the Tax Man.

Here's where the 7702 Plan™ really shines.

Under current IRS tax code, life insurance proceeds are paid out income-tax free. This means they come to the estate, or your family (depending on how the policies are set up) in a lump sum. You can use that money to pay the estate taxes while protecting your other hard-earned assets. Life insurance payouts *are* usually subject to estate taxes, so keep that in mind when you calculate how much insurance you'll need to cover the entire tax bill . . . and as always, consult with a proper estate tax planning professional.

This is where a Safe Money Associate could really help you. Not only can they help you with a 7702 Plan™, but also with asset protection, estate tax planning, and other issues to help build a strategy for protecting and growing your wealth. Just go to:

www.safemoneyretirementbook.com

to request a free 7702 Plan™ Blueprint for Business Owners Only. A Safe Money Associate who has gone through an extensive amount of training on structuring these plans can help you achieve all your goals now to protect your legacy.

FREE BONUS CONTENT

Free 7702 Plan™ Blueprint Analysis Talk with a trained professional who can show you in black and white how to create the financial independence you are looking for.

Lifestyle Income Calculator Discover how long your income will last living the lifestyle you want.

Safe Money For Business Owners See how the 7702 Plan™ can protect your business, build your wealth, and save taxes.

All on: www.safemoneyretirementbook.com

ACKNOWLEDGEMENT

I would like to acknowledge my two associates and friends, Brett Kitchen and Ethan Kap, for their help on this book.

Confidential 7702 Plan™ Blueprint Analysis
(Use black ink, please)

Name: _____

Address: _____

City, State, Zip: _____

Primary Email Address: _____

Day Phone: _____ Evening Phone: _____

Best time to reach you: _____

Were you referred by anyone: _____

Please rate your priorities from 1 to 5 (1 being the most important):

_____ Having an income for life

_____ Keeping your money safely growing outside the market

_____ Having fast access to your money . . . on your terms

_____ Getting out of debt

_____ Financing your own prosperity

To best prepare to help you, please tell us about yourself:

Age: _____

Occupation: _____

Income: _____

Do you own your home? YES or NO

Years left on mortgage:_____ Balance on mortgage: _____

Do you own a business? _____

IMPORTANT: Your information is accessed by Safe Money Associates so they can provide your analysis.

We ask for your phone number and email to be able to provide your 7702 Plan ™ analysis to you. Your Safe Money Associate will design a custom 7702 Plan ™ that may help you reach your financial goals. By filling out and returning this form, you are giving our advisor permission to contact you.

Send your request to:

Safe Money 7702 Plan Blueprint
292 East 12200 South
Draper, UT 84020

ENDNOTES

1   *Federal Reserve Board, 2004*

2   *Cardweb.com*

3   *60 minutes, 401(k) Recession, Ira Rosen*

4   *US News and World Report; 7 Retirement Risks You Need To Prepare for, April 2, 2010. Emily Brandon*

5   *Become Your Own Banker, 2008, Nelson Nash*

6   *FDIC.gov; Foreclosure statistics*

7   *AFL-CIO analysis of 292 companies in the S&P 500 Index. CEO pay data provided by salary.com.*

8   *Barry James Dyke, Pirates of Manhattan*

9   *Nelson Nash, Becoming Your Own Banker*

10   *Barry James Dyke, Pirates of Manhattan*

11   *http://news.bbc.co.uk/2/hi/business/3746044.stm, Monday, 1 November, 2004, news.bbc.co.uk*

12   *http://www.kiplinger.com/magazine/archives/2008/05/hidden- 401(k)-fees.html#ixzz13CwvXJKI*

13   *Damien Hoffman, "Cramer Buy Recommendation CIT Goes Bankrupt," Wall St. Cheat Sheet, Nov. 1, 2009.* 136 Safe Money Millionaire

14   *Bill Alpert, "Cramer's Star Outshines His Stock Picks," Baron's, Feb. 9, 2009.*

15   *Ira Rosen, "The 401(k) Fallout," 60 Minutes*

16   FBI History, Famous Cases, Willie Sutton, *www.fbi.gov*

17   http://www.forbes.com/forbes/2010/0426/investing-obama-taxhikes-capital-gains-duck-obamatax.html

18   Scott Shultz, *www.avoidthedeferraltrap.com*

19   Becoming Your Own Banker, Nelson Nash

20   William Wolman and Anne Colamosca, The Great 401(k) Hoax: Why Your Family's Financial Security Is at Risk and What You Can Do About It (Cambridge, MA: Perseus Publishing, 2002), 12.

21   "The Outer Limits, Some of These Funds Go Way Beyond the Ordinary," Forbes, September 18, 2006.

22   Anthony Mirhaydari, MSN Money The following adapted from Barry James Dyke, The Pirates of Manhattan: Systematically Plundering the American Consumer and How to Protect Against It (Hampton, NH: 555 Publishing, Inc., 2008), 69–76.

23   http://www.livinghistoryfarm.org

24   http://blogs.wsj.com/deals/2010/11/08/tracking-bank-failures- 2010-tops-2009-for-bank-failures/

25   Pirates of Manhattan, Barry James Dyke

26   Ed Slott, The Retirement Savings Time Bomb . . . and how to diffuse it.

27   Based on illustration of 42-year-old male, preferred health, using an A Rated Indexed Life Insurance Company illustration using a 5.7% variable loan rate and 8.7% monthly growth cap.

28   http://finance.yahoo.com/focus-retirement/article/110176/ predicting-your-life-expectancy?mod=fidelityreadytoretire&cat=fidelity_2010_getting _ready_to_retire

29   Adapted from Catherine and Richard Greene, The Man Behind the Magic: The Story of Walt Disney (NY: Viking Penguin, 1991).

30   (Currency/Doubleday, 2005) and Come to the Table: A Celebration of Family Life (Warner Books, 1999).

31   http://www.raricklaw.com/assets/pdf/client-newsroom/2009/

ABOUT THE AUTHOR

Brent Tycksen is the president of a national financial marketing organization with over 70 offices in 30+ states and over 3,000 agents.

Brent has been in the financial services industry since 1978. His passion is helping people grow and protect their wealth from all the financial cancers that afflict us—taxes, market risk, interest exposure, etc.

He and his wife live on a small farm in Salem, Utah, USA where they raise alfalfa, chickens, and beef cattle.

You can contact Brent at:

www.safemoneyretirementbook.com

Made in the USA
San Bernardino, CA
11 February 2014